Dreams, Visions and Fantasies

By Nancy Jean Schmit

Copyright © 2006 by Nancy Jean Schmit

ISBN 978-0-7414-2981-0

Published by:

INFINITY
PUBLISHING.COM

1094 New DeHaven Street, Suite 100
West Conshohocken, PA 19428-2713
Info@buybooksontheweb.com
www.buybooksontheweb.com
Toll-free (877) BUY BOOK
Local Phone (610) 941-9999
Fax (610) 941-9959

Printed in the United States of America

Published January 2014

INDEX

Poetry as a Learning Experience

Dedication

Shelly, you held me up when I didn't feel life was worth living, you taught me the true meaning of friendship and gave me the will to survive. Without you I would not be here today and this book would not have finished. You believed in me when very few did, you understood my pain and heartache.

John F. Harnish my dear sweet friend, I love you dearly. Your support and endless conversations have given me respect for myself, and the encouragement to do what I need to, to survive and be a better person for myself. Life alone can bring so much enjoyment as long as we love ourselves first and listen and learn but most of all do not judge others, you will always be a part of my life and I will carry you closely to my heart, where ever life leads me.

Authors Notes

Please join me on a roller coaster ride of mixed emotions, lost beginnings and cherished endings that have come to me through my own experiences, welcome to my life. Many of my poems are memories that have come to me from my family, loved ones, and from friends past and present. Some of the poems are from deep within my soul, some from my own imagination and many just from wishful thinking.

My book has been developing throughout the years as I struggled through battles within myself. It has also come from the many thoughts that ran rampant through my mind and from emotions felt or repressed, the loves that I will always cherish, losses from which I have learned and hopes and dreams of inner peace.

My words are simple and they are heartfelt and easy to understand, I can promise that many, if not most of you, will be able to relate to my writings. At some point during your reading, my poems might very well become yours. Walk with me through my book and you will feel happiness, love, friendships, family, sadness, death, a will to fight the despair to give up on life.

A portion of my poetry was written in collaboration with many other fine authors and writers online: a group of writers and poets all expressing ourselves in some form or another. I thank them all for allowing me to participate, and for taking me under their wings as I stumbled and learned.

My wishes are that those of you who read my book will find a small portion of yourself in my poems, that you will know that you are not alone in what you feel and that there is hope in each of us to find the love and the answers that lie within our own hearts. I have found strength from my writings and I can only hope that if you are searching for the same strength as me that you find it here, within these pages in which I share my heart and soul with you.

Acknowledgments

There are so very many people throughout my life which deserve recognition somewhere. I am not sure that I could possibly list them all here in this space. I would most like to thank any and all my true friends that kept me on track with my book and all of you that never gave up pushing me to finish it. It may have taken longer than even I thought it would, but to those that had faith in me, you can now see I have accomplished one of my dreams in life.

My parents, who through hard work and constant love taught me so many things. They raised me to love others as I would wish to be loved, to respect people, and especially to work hard through life for what you want, that nothing comes easy. One thing they taught me that I have lived by through life is that family will be there for you even when you don't deserve them to be. There is no greater love than a mother and fathers.

To my children, as a parent and to many other parents out there, we can never be perfect. I tried to learn with you and teach you values that my parents taught me, I now know that I was successful in that matter. The roads ahead of you will not always be smooth, there will be many turns and bumps along the way, but know I will always be here for you, to support and try to understand the best I can. I love you all, and you have been my greatest gift in life. To my Daughter-in-Law Lisa and Grandchildren, Nathan, Austin and Ashley for the great joy you have added to my life, the great gift of love you have brought me. To Dave, I can only hope that our friendship continues through the years ahead and that the love we both share for our children will always be a constant and joyful reminder of the years we spent together.

A very special thank you to my siblings, who stood by me during the roughest stages of my life. Who held my hand and offered there love. I will forever be grateful to you all, and I know you will always offer a helping hand and support when I need it through my journey in life. A special thank you to my sister Sue, her determination, courage and will power to improve herself and her life has overflowed into my life and helped me along the way. I love you all.

Shelly, you kept me sane in a time of my life when very few even knew I existed or cared. You held my hand when I fell deep in depression and offered your home when I needed a place to run to. For six years you continued to give me hope and strength to survive. There are no words I can type that could ever thank you for all you did for me then. I will forever be your friend. To all my online friends that have continued to keep in touch with me over the years and have never forgotten who I am inside and the friendships we shared.

To my dearest friend John F. Harnish, you have kept laughter and enjoyment itself in my life. Your ongoing friendship over the years and your wisdom have shown me a whole different and fun side of life. Because of your encouragement and friendship this book has come to print. Without you I would have given up on a dream, a hope that it would have been possible. You my friend are the one person that believed in me and knew I needed to accomplish this book. No matter where life leads us I know you are only a phone call away. My forever friendship will always be there for you as I know yours will be for me. Until we meet know that I hold you in great respect and love.

To my sweet, sweet friend Sarah, from the first day we met you opened your heart and hands in friendship. I learned so many things in life from you, all of which I still carry through each day. We had some wonderful and memorable times. I love you and your family with all my heart. To my cousin Mark, you proved even when we are at the bottom of the barrel in life we can pull ourselves up and make something good come from our life, thank you and continue your journey with success in life. May you both enjoy life's blessing of Aurora and guide her in her own life's journey.

To Carl, from you I learned it is impossible to please everyone we love. You taught me to not be afraid, to speak from my heart, but most of all you taught me to listen. I shall never forget how you showed me the world or that love comes in many forms through out our lives. You are my best friend and the true meaning of such. A very special thank you for your support and for not allowing me to burn all of these pages when my attitude got the best of me, also for your patience and understanding. Thank you for complimenting my life and standing along side of me through many difficult days and nights, but most of all thank you for listening.

Many thanks go out to Chris, Laura and their family. Nicole, Dylan, Jean, Jim, Bill, Jennifer, Pat, Dan, Tim, Tammy, Jimmy, Randy, Bear, Kim, Herb and their families. To Gary, Joshua, and Paul, through the past 6 or more years you have always respected me, helped me through difficult times, and even when I may have made some wrong choices in life you stayed in touch and cared, thank you very much for your unconditional friendships.

A special thank you to several people that are no longer in my life, but will always hold a piece of my heart and my memories of good times. Gregg Gaither a man that never gave up his fight to survive. my last vision of him laughing on the banks while we were fishing will forever be etched in my mind. Mike-"Ripper" Stephens, the only words I can say that compliment this man are "No Regrets". The music my friend will always play in my home in your memory. Jamie Rieland, a young man that was taken way to soon in life and brought so much laughter into my life. He was like a son to me and I miss him everyday. Scott Rettler, again his life taken at sixteen and he never had the chance to grow to be the wonderful man I know he would have been.

I am most grateful to Infinity Publishing for bringing my words into print and allowing me to express myself in ways that sometimes I don't even understand, and for taking the time and patience in helping me bring my words all together instead of a scrambled mess of papers along side my computer.

Thanks to all those who have bought my book, and for taking the time to read my writings. I hope a piece of me follows through each page and brings some form of enjoyment and heartfelt feelings to your day.

Praise from Nancy's readers

Nancy's poetry has always given me something to think over in my life's paths. Nancy I am so happy for you in the publishing of your poetry, congratulations.

Gary Chicago, III

Dear Reader,

Congratulations! You have in your hands a book of poems that has taken many years of good and difficult times to complete. Nancy and I first met in 1998 and quickly became good online friends. During those 6 plus years, we have been through many ups and downs in our lives and, with the help and support of each other, have become stronger and more positive in our attitudes and out-looks on life. Her poetry exemplifies some of those good and bad times in her life and I share with you in the happiness of her publi-cation of this work of love.

Paul A. Krusac, Michigan-Texas

Your talents are so unbelievable and I am so happy that you have accomplished one of your many dreams. You have inspired me to be who I am and be myself, no matter what others think or believe.

I Love You

Kerry Brockman, Wisconsin

Dear Readers,

This book that you hold in your hands is not only an amazingly beautiful compilation of poems but the very heart and soul of a very special friend of mine. On days when she could not voice her emotions to anyone, Nancy would bare her soul in the form of a poem. Nancy shared her works for many, many years with very few and I was always lucky enough to be among the chosen few. Her poems will take you through a roller coaster of emotions, may they be unnervingly sad or exhilaratingly happy you will find you yourself in many of her poetic offerings. Please enjoy this special gift that Nancy has decided to share with the world and open yourself to the love she has to offer. (Moon, all I have to say to you is "YOU GO GIRL"!! We ALL told you that you COULD do it!! ILY)

Shelly~

California

What a wonderful accomplishment for my Sister. Knowing Nancy, and what she has experienced, I look forward to reading her life through the words of her poetry. Congratulations and I'm proud of you!!

Susie

A Letter To My Love

My Dearest Love.
Your eyes hold me spellbound while
your soul imprisons and strangles mine,
making two souls into one,
sip through the glass of life with me,
toast to an eternity of friendship we share,
savor the taste upon our lips,
our desire and temptations,
an endless love swirled in crystal,
with the incense of passion.
You smile and I begin to melt away,
your soft spoken words nourish thoughts within me,
I give to you what you truly deserve,
my sequestered heart and soul.
My everlasting promise to love you forever.
No words I can ever write could capture
what I feel when you hold me tight,
and when you whisper "I love You."
Your love pours into my heart like a fine wine from a crystal goblet.
Your intimate touches, the fire of passion,
your faithfulness and honesty.
Please wrap me within your strong embrace,
releasing a feeling so great,
complimenting my life.

Acceptance

Years of destructive thoughts within myself
kept me in deep despair,
doubts and insecurities are not worth the pain
I carried for so long.
The weight heavy upon my shoulders.

Years of grief and shame,
self doubt and no self esteem,
I came to realize that I have
only myself to blame.

Human hearts are fragile and blind,
and sometimes we can't see
what we need to.
It takes strength and effort within
to cease negative thoughts and find self worth
security and the love of ourselves.

I will no longer let the demons haunt me,
or keep my heart in darkness,
I hold my head up freely
and look at my faults directly,
I love myself just the way I am.

Another Day

As another day sets into the distance,
she again sits alone with only her written words for comfort.
Many days go by that she wonders with exhausting efforts
why one person that has so much love and so much heart to give
can feel so much hurt.
Does she allow this pain to take control of her,
does she allow her soul and heart to be crushed so freely again,
would the answer be to be less giving, less open,
or does she continue to be the person she was raised to be and hope
that someday one single human being will see her cries
and feel her loving heart so open to all.
Do all the salty tears her eyes shed have a purpose,
are they teaching her the way to true love of herself,
showing her mistakes and failures,
reminding her of the love she offered to others.
She looks into the words of this woman,
she searches her being, will she find out who she really is.
If she allows herself to open up and look
will she finally see what so many have told her about herself,
the person that she wants to be but does not see,
or will she continue to build her walls higher
until they collapse in on her.
What does she have to lose, she already cannot breath, the walls
she has built are crushing her.
She sits in tears and anger,
fear of giving herself and her love to another,
fear of pain again to unbearable to go on.
She reads her own words and knows her soul is waiting to escape
into blue sun filled skies,
her wings again open to the world outside of the walls she built.
What she holds inside those walls is only destroying her.
Let her smile, let her sing out a wonderful melody.

5

See her words of pure innocence and yet feel also what her past
has made her.
Do not hurt this fragile butterfly, for she has kept her heart from
flight for to long,
as tomorrow morning brings the sun, rising in a brilliant warm
glow, she shall stretch out her wings again and like a young bird
learning to fly she will stumble and fall, but she will not give up
until she soars high into the wind.
Let that wind carry her, then she will be able to find herself.
When you see her drifting beautifully by you
please hold out your hand and allow her to land
you will find no other that will love you as she will,
for there are very few of us left in this world,
as the wild birds we have
become extinct in a world of greed, wealth and self destruction.

A Single Tear Forms

Have you ever watched a tear form?
It starts as a small pool in the eye,
as pain and sorrow increases in volume
so does the pool.
Finally filled to maximum level and overflows,
running gently down the cheek,
dropping off to never exist again.

Each tear having its own character,
its own short life,
even an individual form of its own.
Once fallen it is gone forever,
short lived, but it did exist.

Do we ever wonder what
brought this tear to form?
If in slow motion we watched as it formed
and took its route, would we see the purity of it?
A colorless form, tasteless,
untouched by human hands.
How can something so beautiful be
created from pain and hurt?

So many of us try to hide them,
they are really the most purest part of us,
the most vulnerable and innocent.
We hold them back,
we fight them,
we wipe them so not to be seen,
is it fair that we do not share them
or let others see the true beauty of them,
for in one brief second its beauty, its existence,
is gone forever.

Attic Of Memories

People tend to hide memories and their family history
like old toys or antique furniture in an attic,
so far away, out of site,
many stairs to climb to find them.

Their hopes, their dreams,
memories of relatives past,
photographs of good times,
memories that could enhance their life,
make them laugh with joy.

Take them down and enjoy them,
remember the hugs, the kisses,
the laughter of young children,
your junior prom, your first date,
the dresser your grandmother stored
her linens in.

Enjoy the memories from the past,
the thoughts and wishes you had,
all of those memories hidden,
stored away in boxes or and old trunk.
In a dark place where no one can see,
where you cannot enjoy and cherish.

Boxes filled and covered in dust,
cobwebs hanging,
framed pictures of distant relatives,
what beauty so many hide in dark places.

Explore those dark closets,
those hidden boxes,
let your children learn of past history and family,
teach them what values hold in the attic.
An attic of Hidden memories.

"FIRST FLIGHT"

Beautiful Soul

Her soul is one of simple beauty,
to me she is timeless.
Her soul and heart reflect in the eyes and lives
of small helpless creatures.
She dwells on her own mistakes and flaws,
not realizing the perfection so many around her see.
Her heart reaches out to failing lives,
to the homeless creatures of the world.
She covers her own pain and heartache
with the joys of helping others.
A beautiful woman locked in her own prison.
She feels she is nothing,
to me she is everything I dream I could be.
She feels she is worthless,
but to all the lives she saves,
and those of us who know her she is priceless.
She talks of being worn out,
but she keeps stepping forward and giving.
She is beautiful, yet she will never know to what extent.
She does not know how my heart lights up when
we speak, or how her smile lights up a room.
She drowns in her own tears,
but never stops giving of herself,
even when she feels she has no more to give.
She is priceless to me,
priceless to all the tiny lives she saves,
she is my strength when I have none of my own,
the strength of dying creatures
when they fail to have their own.
She is my wisdom when my mind fails to make sense.
Her heart beats for mine when my own wants to stop.
She is my dearest friend,
and I love her.

No matter what accomplishments you make,
somebody else helped you.

Althea Gibson

The Blade

Across my wrist,
I trace a path the blade will take,
do I dare end it this way,
let those that love me
find me laying in a pool of
my own blood.

So filled with fear
of what life has in store for me,
it's hard to see the path I have drawn my
eyes filled with tears,
I have cried and cried for so very long,
all alone, the pain others do not see.

My mind and body numb
to all the world around me,
I feel the sting of the blade as it
slides across my wrist,
I flinch but know the pain will not last.

Watching as the blood flows,
small droplets as they explode in
different directions as they hit the floor
beneath me.

All the pain I held inside,
the worries of disappointing those I love,
start to fade away.
I betrayed myself and those around me
I'll never forget you,
or those I have left behind.

Can they forgive me for what I am about to do,
I guess I'll never know,
it is too late to stop the blood that flows.
It takes my fears and pain,
this blade of death is just a
means for me to forget.

Caged Bird

My feelings you were never aware,
I can assure you they were always there,
its hard to breath,
to close my eyes and only think of mistakes,
mistakes we both made.
It is hard to live my life when I feel I am so all alone,
it is impossible to go forward
when I feel so out of control,
trapped and caged like a bird without wings,
unable to explore or fly to greater heights.
Captured by my own ignorance of people
of life outside my own little world.
A world not only created by me,
but created by you and all those that surrounded us.
Living a life they created,
a life they expected us to live,
what society expected.
Letting all this take control of my dreams,
my plans for my life,
a hypnotic trance one may say,
walking through life in what others thought was best,
what they thought I should be and do.
Caged in the morals and the beliefs of others,
unable to think for myself,
unable to open my wings,
open the gate and fly free.

Capture The Beauty

There is so much beauty in the world,
if only each of us could stop,
look, and take the time to notice it,
to capture it in our minds.

Wouldn't it be wonderful to take the
beauty of a warm sun,
let it travel in zig zag directions until it
finds the good in all of us,
then in one instant it bursts through,
exploding knowledge and warmth
to those unfortunate that live in darkness.
We all know we cannot touch such beauty
without overflowing it to others,
it lies within each one of us,
if taken the right directions we can
let it burst and explore so many others.

A great beauty waiting
to touch the souls of so many
in need of even the smallest glow.

Look within yourself and find that
small glow, share it with those that do
not have faith or knowledge of life's beauty
Look within yourself and know
a small part of you gave that beauty to one other person.

Cherish Every Moment

Special times in our lives are fleeting,
like footprints in the freshly fallen snow,
we never know for sure if we will see the sun rise
as we lay our heads to rest each night.

We must cherish every moment we have,
time goes by to quickly,
understand its worth, and never regret.
We each have paths to follow,
and loved ones to hold dear,
never take for granted that they
will always be there.

Someday my sun will not rise,
my journey on earth will end.
I have lived each moment,
my heart filled with memories and love,
I have given freely and openly my friendship,
cared for those I have met,
I have no regrets.
The mistakes I have made through life
I believe have all been forgiven,
so I can say I will cherish every moment
and let none slip away.

Choices She Made

She is sorry they had to suffer and hurt,
that their tears fell silent.
She knows it was just a matter of time,
she had to make choices which in time kept her alive.

Some were very painful, and they hurt many she loves.
So often she wishes her choices
did not have to cause so much pain.
She does not regret them,
she only regrets the hurt they caused.

She knows she was never the perfect partner,
nor the perfect mother,
she just wants those she loves to know that she did try.

Feeling as if she could not continue,
hurting so deeply inside,
never imagining a breakdown,
or guessed she would cry the many tears she cried.

Not wishing to live another day,
time just seemed to stand still,
and all her confusion was still there.

Her life has since opened,
new experiences, inner understanding of herself,
new friendships, new places.

She has found the person she wished to be,
the person she thought was lost forever.
Grown past the anger and hurt, hoping someday
all those she loves will see a wiser
and stronger person.

Confusion

Broken heart and torment,
from there to here to there again,
following her wherever she goes,
every gesture or process she goes through,
affecting her in every way,
a heart filled with sorrow,
a mind with confusion,
and a soul that endures all the pain,
weak from all it holds.
She looks for peace, searches for endurance,
can her mind, soul, heart, and body all reunite,
giving her spirit and hope again?

I have a simple philosophy. Fill what's empty.
Empty what's full. And scratch where it itches.

Alice Roosevelt Long worth (1884-1980)
Socialite and wit

Construction

I once considered myself a condemned house.
Walls falling in, beams cracked and rotted,
every room you entered weak and filthy,
dust and dirt covering each entry,
then I found you.

Offering a hand in friendship,
words of constructive views,
strength to support my weakness,
slowly rebuilding each fallen wall.
Dusting off old fragile memories,
closing up each hole one by one.

Turning dark filthy windows into sparkling panes
of glass that allowed sunshine in.
Sweeping the past into darkness.
Building my confidence and self esteem,
each day restoring what was once so beautiful inside,
merging our souls together as one.

You are my strength and foundation,
you have reconstructed my heart,
given new life to a condemned existence.
Restored and improved what once was falling
and rotting from the inside out.

Clear sunshine and star filled windows,
pictures of sunsets and aqua waters hang from each memory,
laughter filling every hallway,
painted walls of brilliant colors,
and a roof that no longer leaks weakness or rainfall.

Dancing Images

My heart sings aloud
with the sound of your voice.
Images of two dancing
through the nights moonlight,
our bodies interweaving
as the night passes by,
two as one,
dancing as if time has stopped,
my lips have felt the pleasure of yours,
the sweet taste of perfection.
Fingers entwined into your
masculine and strong hands,
leading my heart with tenderness,
a touch as gentle to my face as the wings
of a white dove passing.
You trace my curves with a delicate whisper,
fingers exploring wrist to elbow,
stomach to breast,
downward the full length of my body,
stirring the passions within me.
The sensual sound of your voice
draws me into another world,
silken comfort, sensual desires,
calm peaceful existence,
drawn in a heavy spiral out of control,
deeper, deeper into your soul.

Do Not

Do not judge me for my faults, we all have many.
I am not without error.
Do not cry for me,
for I cry enough for many.
My tears are no different than yours.
Do not compare me to others,
I am unique in my own way. Each of us are.
Do not assume you know me,
if you have not taken the time to explore my inner
self being and soul.
Do not hold my heart in your hands if you are
going to crush it with your strength, or try to replace
it with your beliefs, I have my own.
Do not twist my thoughts to make them yours,
or to make them what you feel is right.
They may not be right for you,
but they are for me.
Do not cast that first stone in my direction
unless you are willing to look beyond
my mistakes and see your own.
That stone may grow in size and change direction.
Do not make me the center of your jokes,
or ridicule me for my differences,
Laughter is meant to warm the heart not to tear someone's apart.
Do not preach to me right and wrong until you
can look at your own life and find no mistakes.
I doubt anyone can.
Do not forgive me for my mistakes in life,
forgive yourself for yours,
I bare enough of my own to forgive.

Do not paint a distorted picture of my life,
and let the world see it through your eyes,
unless you are willing and able to do the same with your own.
It may surprise you at the abstract design or the lack
of color and brightness.
We are all individuals, we all make mistakes,
we all make choices, some we regret.
Our life is not one color nor is it perfect without fault,
Do not judge others until you can take time
and look at your own.

Earth Awakening

The sizzling sun on the ocean,
a hot brightness being replaced by moonlight,
trees rustling as the wind brushes past,
crickets singing, attracting their mates,
blackness overtakes,
the mysterious moon forcing its glow,
a chilly evening air replacing
the suns sizzling rays,
but the moon smiles,
sparkling on sleeping grass,
soon the sun will dominate once again,
the constant changing of earth's lessons,
eternity within our reach.

Embracing Every Moment

The night is bitter cold,
she lay still beneath the covers,
waiting for him to come home.
He will lay his head beside her,
pulling her tightly into his arms,
she will feel safe there, secure,
not knowing any harm or insecurities.
She embraces every moment she has with him,
whispering the love she feels for him,
a gentle kiss upon her lips,
passion releasing from his fingertips to her flesh.
Music playing faintly in the background,
their eyes locked on each other,
hearts feeling each others melody,
dancing in perfect rhythm
beneath the sheets that cover them lightly.
The heat and passion of their bodies taunting each other,
they become one single entity,
no beginning and no end.
The sweetness of her lips linger upon his,
the smell of her body tantalizes his senses,
Never again will she let him know the feeling of a cold and lonely
bed.
They fade into a sweet joyous slumber,
wrapped in each others arms,
exhausted, loved, comforted,
but never again will they feel empty inside,
alone without passion or love to fill their nights.

Erotic Episode

They sit on the sofa closely,
her head resting gently on his shoulder,
he intently watches the movie
smiles and pleasure adorn his face.
She searches for her own sense of pleasure,
her hand brushes gently across his lap,
She looks upward to see if he notices'.
His slight evil smile obviously a sign he does.
Her hand stops and a slight bit of arousal
and pressure puts him on the edge of his seat,
slowly moving her hand,
each movement perfectly in rhythm with his,
He leans back letting her take control and
ignoring the movie,
a satisfaction and delight cross his face,
his heart begins beating rapidly and
his breathing becomes hard and fast.
Her grip becomes firmer and her pace quickens,
her thumb rubbing gently over his
most sensitive member.
His eyes glaze over with intense pleasure,
fingers forming into a fist,
his palms are sweating and his grip
is overexcited.
suddenly the climaxing moment sends waves of
warmth and pure ecstasy through his body,
She looks into his eyes as he tries desperately to
catch his breath, searching for the right words,
she falls softly onto his chest, holding one another closely.
Pure excitement, pleasuring him,
no words spoken, his look is all she needed.
A sly smile slides over her lips,
an evil giggle hints of her satisfaction.

Eyes

You may not hear them speak
but if you look deep within them they tell all.
What a heart holds,
what a soul feels,
and what the mind thinks.

They are simple but in the same
aspect very complicated.
At times, dark as a stormy cloud above,
at times filled with the brightest sparkle,
for all is held within one glance.

Look beyond their color,
their beauty or sadness,
see deep inside,
it is then you will see that persons
inner beauty.

There may very well be many obstacles
in your way,
and there may yet to be one living soul
who has accomplished the maze,
if you take the challenge and time
once you enter you will never leave.
For one's eyes hold all the truth,
all the beauty that very few take the time to truly explore.

My Fathers Home

As a young child in my fathers home
I remember the smell of grease as he would come home
from work each night.
The tiredness in his eyes as he would sit down at the dinner table,
there was this silence at our table,
my father was a stern man, and as his children we had this fear of
him,
I am not sure today why we did
we always knew his love for us.
Our home looked like a palace,
but we were far From rich with material things.
Our parents raised us with the riches so few today know,
a family bond of love, respect, and caring hearts.
The spring would come and the garden work needed to be done,
side by side as a family we planted each seed to grow.
Sirens would blow for help in our small town,
my father would rush off to do what he could,
the pride that I felt I cannot explain, even as young as I was
I remember I was so deathly scared,
what if something happened to him while he helped others.

You may ask why I write these words of my father,
you see, for the first time I see my father growing old and weak,
his health failing. Today I seen him cry for the first time,
he hugged me goodbye and gave me a gentle kiss,
he sent me off with his love.
I didn't want to let go,
for it was something I so desperately longed for since childhood.
He was never one to say I love you.

Today I heard those words and for the first time
I truly felt my fathers love.
There are times I feel I have let him down,
but I know even if I have he still is proud of me.

I called my father today, for the first time in my life
I did not feel that small child within me escaping once again,
He did not judge me, or lecture me.
As I said my good-byes I felt tears slowly stream down my cheeks,
I so desperately wanted his hug once again.
It is odd to me that it took half my life to know that feeling,
I will thank God for giving me my fathers hug that day,
I shall never be to old to feel the love of his arms wrap around me.

I Love You Dad

"FLYING FREE"

Fly Free Like An Eagle

Spread your arms outward like an eagles wings,
fly high, soar over the tree tops,
feel the warmth of the sun.
Fly free like an eagle my love,
leave time stand still for a moment
and search for the unknown,
let the wind take hold of your flight
and guide your graceful wings amidst the sky.
Look upon the earth below
leaving all your problems behind.
Fly my love, take your freedom and explore
the world beyond these walls I have trapped you in.
Take flight, high above the bluffs and trees,
like an injured bird I tried to heal your wounds,
I did not succeed in that task.
Fly free like the great eagle,
I shall set you free from the confined places of my heart
and release you into flight.
Fly free my friend, my love,
its where you are meant to be.
Fly Free.

Forever In My Heart

You were hand picked to be my parents,
there is no one else that can ever fill
your place within my heart.
I know there have been times
that I have failed to see how very much
you have done for me,
and how you've always given me your best.

I need to tell you how very much I have grown,
you have placed my needs above
any needs of your own.
You have been my teacher of the world
my best friend through life,
given me the gift of giving and loving.
The gift of a forever love of parents.

I am thankful most of all for you Mom,
much more than words can ever say.
All my life you have given me all of your love,
and I now know your love has guided me
through many difficult times.
Our souls, our hearts,
our lives are bond together,
that bond can never be broken, and
it will never stray.

Just as I turn to make my way
I turn and see the love shine through
both of your eyes, nothing is said,
no other words need be spoken,
our spirits free
Forever and a day.

Forgiveness

A gift of cleansing the soul,
a single act of forgiveness,
is worth more than all the silver
and gold in the world.

What we give each other in time
and money is noble at best,
but nothing pleases the heart
like forgiveness.

When we can learn to forgive
we can learn to love ourselves,
forgiveness adds joy to our
every existence in life.

Gentle Friendships

In the course of life,
we are never sure just what a day may bring us.
We can never be completely sure of any one thing,
we cannot be sure of what discomforts we may face.
The only thing we can be sure of is that our hearts be true,
songs may be left with no melody, words left unspoken,
sometimes we have a lot to face,
doubt may enter in, but always let your heart
be filled with love, peace and forgiveness.
Tomorrow holds an unseen path for all of us,
sometimes it feels like an uphill climb with no ending,
let friendships ease each step,
hold my hand and let me guide you through the day,
through life we all shed tears,
we laugh at life's silly quirks,
remember that the moon will always rise,
the morning sun will always shine,
tomorrow my friend is one step closer to our climb to the top.
Silently we will forever be friends, our friendship has
with stood many hard times, it spans many miles apart,
I shall be there always for you,
I know you will always and forever be there for me.
If not in person, in spirit and in love.
No matter what tomorrow brings either of us,
or where our paths may lead,
the two of us shall meet some day.
When you gaze upon the night sky tonight
know that I too am looking in your direction
and sending through the stars my wishes and
my forever friendship.

Laughter is the shortest distance between two people.

Victor Borge

Hang On And Seize It

Visual memories,
touchable thoughts,
unfortunately so.
Disappearing with time,
tasteful kisses,
diminishing pain,
weakened heart,
negative promises,
torn apart emotions,
exhausted relationship,
taught to hide,
battle wounds unseen,
unheard,
strangers,
knowledge found to much,
obligations,
huge intrusion,
confusion,
demands, commands so great,
pitiful eyes crying,
helpless,
doubtful gloomy days,
sleepless nights,
unrealistic images,
desires, hopes,
love decaying, trapped,
new world awakening,
escaping, running,
digging in deeper,
crawling forward,
climbing out,
looking around,
inspiration found,
freedom within,
hang on seize it.

Happy Fathers Day Dad

As the wind whispers through the fresh
buds of springtime,
a scent of rain mixed lightly with the
fragrance of lilacs and newly cut grass,
I walk quietly, barefoot as I did when I was a young child.
As an adult, the child you knew then
still exists within me.
That child cries aloud at times wishing once again for
Daddy's arms to take away her pain,
Your strength to once again carry me through another day.
I follow the path that my life has lead me too.
The memories I will carry forever,
with hundreds of miles separating us I can feel your love
guide me each day.
I hear your words gently blowing past me in the wind,
"All is for a reason my child, with each season that passes
you will find faith, happiness, and love within yourself."

I sit quietly watching the sun set and the stars beginning to shine
brightly,
the vision of your smile shines amongst them
and the wind once again turns to whispers of your voice to me.
"hold on little girl, hold on tightly to your beliefs,
your soul is of beauty, caring and loving little girl.
and old soul. I cannot give you answers little one,
I can only be there when you ask me to be."

Father I ask myself so many times would you be proud
of the woman I have become. I find my answer to be
that of one I need ask myself first.
"Am I proud of who I am?"

Seldom I have told you this Dad,
with tears slowly falling against my cheeks,
the night air becoming cool and damp,
I close my eyes and I feel your presence
and on this night I make a vow to myself to tell you
as often as I can how very much I love You.

You Taught Me To Love Again

Words can never express
the feelings that I hold for you.
The special times you have given me,
the shine that radiates from your eyes when we speak,
like glistening gold in the river as the suns rays catch it.

I can never repay you for all you have given me,
your trust, your love,
the security I feel as I lay falling asleep in your arms,
the love you have shown me,
words alone could never be enough to express how
I feel inside for you.

When I needed you the most, your heart
opened to me,
your arms stretched out wide,
and you gave me more than anyone ever has.
You have taught me patience, understanding,
self respect, but most of all
faith in who I am and that I can be loved unconditionally.

The tears we have shed together
will forever remind me of your gentleness,
I have witnessed a side of you
that I believe very few have taken the
time or heart to see.
My love for you is endless,
and best friends we shall always be.

He Keeps Me Safe

He took me into his open arms,
he held me close and safe
protecting me from hurt, from myself.
brought laughter into my life once more.
He shields me from pain,
watches over me as I sleep,
his love for me is soothing,
his inner light seeps through me
igniting a fire inside my soul,
he holds me tightly never
letting me go,
he holds me in his saving arms
and it is here in his world,
his arms, I wish to stay forever.

Her Mirror Image

She walks with grace,
the clapping echo of her shoes
heard for miles as she walks towards her reality.
Her head hanging low,
eyes fixed on every step she makes,
mind wandering into insane thought.

For one brief moment she stops,
looking into the plate glass window of the store,
her image she sees so differently than which others see,
she stands in amazement at herself,
how easily it is to hide all we feel inside,
how easily we can add a hat or a certain dress
and our image to others changes.

It is only through her eyes she truly sees herself,
for she is the only one that knows
the pain she holds within,
if you see her standing there,
you see a small frame with a glow and a smile,
she sees an aged woman in tattered clothes,
wrinkles deep from worry,
eyes blackened from restlessness,
a heart filled with emptiness,
her soul fading in time.

Now look again,
do you now see the difference.

Her Own Pleasure

Her eyes close to sweet thoughts of passion,
so intense she can feel the warmth of his breath,
the moisture of his lips tracing the form of her neck,
his hand brushing her hair from her face.
His body forcing itself against hers
so tightly it takes her breath away.
Her hands exploring her own contour,
leaving her with more desire for him.
She lay motionless imagining him laying there beside her.
The scent of his raw flesh filling the room,
his lips tracing down her sides,
a kaleidoscope of colors spinning through her mind.
Her own thoughts bringing a passion so intense,
sweat beads upon her pale flesh
as she feels him enter her body.
It is then that she shudders within,
she begins to convulse in his embrace,
gripping the sheets beneath her
collapsing in her own fantasy as she lay staring
at the ceiling above.
She is not ashamed of thoughts of him,
sometimes she finds herself on the verge of obscene,
sometimes in a land of unknown.
She goes to places where she has control,
where she teaches herself how to please.

Advice is what we ask for when we already know the answer but wish we didn't.

Erica Jong

Passion

Candle light sparkles within your brown eyes,
my desire to feel your touch burns inside me,
the warmth of your body against my skin,
fingers lightly stroking my hair,
taking me to a different place and time.

Your hands so gentle and tender,
in your arms I become lost,
gazing upon your face,
feeling as if I do not know you,
looking into your eyes, deep,
seeing pain, a lost life to
your own doing at times,
a ravens eyes.

Your lips, your tongue,
soft and wet as they meet mine,
passion in our souls,
desire in our hearts,
the moment is ours, take control.
You cease to amaze me,
olive skin tone,
loving, wise beyond my beliefs,
was it born in your blood
or did the years teach you.

Driving me wild,
wanting to stay forever,
I can't let you go, or would I wish to,
non-existent without you, destined to be
complete with you.
Passionate only for you.

His Evilness Lurks

She lay silently,
sheets of elegant spun silk beneath her,
shear fabric hung from above,
flowing delicately around her bed,
cascading to the floor,
exposing the full moons erotic glare.

Her mind enhanced with visions,
she lay motionless,
a vine of flowers slowly entwines her body,
her deep darkened hair covered with their beauty.
Hypnotized with the glow of the moon glaring through her window,
she lay there in a trance.

Slowly the mixture of scents from the flowers
drifts her off into a peaceful state of mind.
Her glazed green eyes close,
the perfect picture of beauty lay before him,
no other eyes can see her,
no other hands may touch her,
she is his.

His evil laughter heard from behind the closed door.
The spell he placed upon her lips has taken hold,
her body, her mind, her soul,
captured with one poisonous kiss.
He controls her dreams her thoughts,
her every breath.
In one simple second he takes it all from her,
The control of her mind is so easily taken.

He is the devil and he feeds off greed,
guilt, wrong doings.
He walks the earth in darkness,
taking control of the weak,
giving him one small edge and she shall be his,
he shall take over her life.

Pen In Hand

So often I sit with pen in hand,
writing of dreams and expectations,
there are times words flow easily from my fingertips,
and times no words seem to fit together at all,
a poets true frustration.
I read of love lost,
of love found,
sunsets and rainy days,
pain in others hearts,
smiles perched upon their lips,
eyes swollen from tears they have shed.

Many words written by people I have never seen,
but words written I feel everyday.
If so many that write feel as I,
what do those who do not write feel,
and is it the same.

A basket of collective thoughts
I surely could write today,
but instead I think I will pray for
all the souls that touch me each day,
and for those yet to be heard.

As I put down my pen
I clasp my hands in prayer,
asking to warm the hearts of those
saddened today and to dry their tears.
Let those who cannot find the words, write.

If not on paper then in their minds,
let them find answers, let them find friendships,
or just let them find a friend that
shares their thoughts, their ideas,
their caring hearts, let them find that friend
as I have.

Looking Into His Eyes

Looking into his eyes she learned that through them
she would find herself again.
As he held her in his arms,
music was playing quietly in the background,
it was then she knew all her wishes,
fantasies and yearnings had become reality.
The only words she could speak were,
"Thank You."

The very essence of his body next to hers
moving slowly to music unknown, is almost overwhelming,
She wants to taste his every syllable,
feel the warmth of his breath on her neck.
She can see an endless world of happiness,
an unexplainable view of peace and tranquility.

Her heart which had been tightly locked found him,
he now holds the only key.
This feeling which is so overwhelming and powerful
cannot be explained,
in his eyes she can see forever.

She bathed in his comfort and essence,
as he translates his feelings, swaying to the rhythm of the music.
Without a word spoken he has completed her life.
As the song comes to and end, she again looked into his eyes,
and it was then she heard them speak to her.
"I Love You."

"SPRINGTIME IN WISCONSIN"

Hidden Child Within Her

A young child hiding in this grown woman's' body.
her cries sometimes escaping, piercing screams.
She holds a golden pen,
writing her words of love found, and love lost,
desperation, anguish.

Holding onto the small child within her
keeps the beauty of a happier time.
A place in her past where no pain or hurt existed,
where only laughter of a small fragile soul ran free.
Warm summer rain falling lightly,
small figures running, twirling in circles,
arms reaching to the sky,
a tender and simple soul.
to be that child again and feel that kind of freedom,
hearing a child's laughter,
wishing that she had never had to face so much turmoil,
the slow destruction of one so innocent and free.

Grown she sees her past before her,
feels all the tears she shed,
all the pain and hurt she endured through many years,
realizing that child's innocent soul is still inside her,
the faith and the morals have not been destroyed
they have just been temporarily taken from her,
can she finally release that child, and grow
to be the woman she wishes to be?

"MEMORIES"

Silent Skies

The darkness falls and the sky is clear,
stars shining in brilliant colors and shapes,
I sit here feeling as if the world is swallowing me alive,
fighting to breath, to exist,
trying to find myself in a world of shallow people.

I fall back onto the sandy ground beneath me,
taking a deep breath,
the days seeming so long and so empty,
the air so warm on my pale skin.

As the wind begins to blow through the trees
I feel a coldness run through me,
another day alone,
with only the silence of the skies above.

If only it could speak to me,
guide me in the direction I need to go,
one star leading to another, showing me,
taking me down the path I need.

As I open my eyes the sun is rising
the moon has since fallen to daybreak,
and no path, no direction,
still alone and uncertain,
searching once again.

She Stands Afraid

Her heart torn by him,
she stands alone and afraid,
afraid of once again letting go.
He speaks of being sorry,
of making mistakes,
how he never meant to make her cry,
or how he never meant to hurt her.
She stands afraid of loving him,
she can feel his love for her,
she knows that love is real,
but she stands afraid.
Can she forgive him for being untrue to her heart,
she feels emptiness, lost,
so very numb inside.
How can he say this is love,
is it at all possible.
Can she reach for the stars and for her dreams,
or has he destroyed even those.
She stands afraid once again,
her heart scared to love,
scared to trust.

Should It Be

If the day comes that I grow weak,
and I can no longer sleep,
or the day comes that pain
takes control and it no longer
allows me to enjoy life,
let your love for me guide you
to do what needs to be done,
for you will know when my battle
can no longer be won.

I know you will be hurting,
and that I promise I understand,
we have had so many wonderful
times together,
some with laughter and others with tears,
but I know you would not want to suffer,
so I now ask you,
let your love for me with stand the ultimate test.

Stay with me until the end,
hold me tightly and whisper soft
thoughts to me,
Let me feel your touch as my eyes
close and I no longer can see,
let me feel your breath against my skin,
do not grieve for me, but don't let
your heart hold back it's sadness.

Watch as my soul drifts off
to a place where it will now be free,
do not fear this time,
let me go, remember my smile,
and your love I held so dear,
let them guide you through.

Midnight Candle

Midnight, candles burning,
red blazing fire,
speak to her with oranges and yellows,
reds of passion and desire.

Midnight, candles burning,
red flaming hear,
Seek out the one that holds her heart,
burn her lips with ecstasy.

Midnight candles burning,
hand grasping tilting
hot wax dripping,
tantalizing her flesh.

Midnight candles burning,
red blazing fire,
speak to her with heat,
speak to her desires.

Midnight candles burning,
finish what you started,
flickering red hot wick,
reaching it's end,
reaching her ultimate climax.

Scars

Sitting here all alone,
thoughts of leaving and finding a new home,
The scars of years gone past,
the tears I would leave behind,
leaving all monetary things you gave me,
leaving all my fears.
I have walked towards the door so many times,
packed my things and started walking away.
This time I open the door,
bags packed, car open,
I locked the past as I shut the door,
I say a silent prayer and take a brief look
as I drive off.
I pray that I will find peace and happiness,
that those I am leaving behind will forgive me,
I pray that my family will be safe,
that my choice will not hurt them,
I don't know where this will lead me,
but I know I will find myself,
and I know it will make me stronger.
I will finally be free from the hurt.
I only want to be happy and have hope,
life has its changes, but he will not change,
all my pleas and cries went unheard.
The road ahead seems so long,
I do not know where I am going but I know
I must live, and I must find answers.

Molecule Of Desire

The morning sun rises in the eastern sky,
his coffee in hand he sits at his desk.
The screen blinks on,
his thoughts are not that of work or numbers,
a portrait of her etched in his thoughts,
not a woman of great beauty,
her body not flawless by any means,
it is not that which she prays he witnessed.
Life experiences she has endured,
the beauty she holds beneath all exterior,
the kiss she offers sweet, tender seductive,
a lick upon his lips with the taste of morning dew,
the twirling of her fingers through his hair at the base of his neck,
his hair hugging her fingers each twirl bringing him closer to her,
careening to places where their joining felt infinite.
The quiet fight in his mind returns to his screen,
without hesitation he finds his mind once more capturing visions of
her,
her legs tangled in thin sheets as she sleeps before him,
the sound of soft instrumental music in the background,
leading his thoughts to the night before, what consumes him now
desire,
carefully he searches the contour of her body with his eyes,
a mystery of sweetness yet to be tasted by his lips,
the softness of her fair skin wanting his gentle touch to seduce her,
in the silence he can hear her breathing,
smell her fragrance that illuminates the room
wild flowers delicate to his senses.
Her eyes closed in sleep, her heartbeat echoing,
he lies next to her as to not disturb her, his arms wrap around her,
in that instant her legs wrap tightly around him, his hands cover her
breasts,
eyes now open and meeting with the seductive stare of his,
no words are uttered, their hands begin to talk through caressing,

the two of them listen only to their fingertips, they feel every mole-
cule of desire,
sudden moistening, the deep aching within them both,
the need for pleasure which has risen.
Their bodies entwine as one,
climbing to a passion neither have ever known,
continuous arousal of senses and desires long past the evening
hours.
He rests inside her, their legs still wrapped loosely around each
other,
her flesh scorched by an unmeasured pleasure,
she willingly gave herself to him,
so easily their passions have found contentment.

Anxiety is a thin stream of fear trickling through the mind. If encouraged, it cuts a channel into which all other thoughts are drained.

Arthur Somers Roche (1883-1935)
Novelist and playwright

In Spirit And Need

I want to make a difference in your life,
in spirit and in need.
I want your life to shine so bright
and burn inside of me.

I want the world to look at you
and see the love of me,
that all I am reflects
from within your eyes.

May all the love I give you
be a legacy for you.
May it guide you through the future,
and forever carry you .

Let the words of love I offer
and the gentleness of my touch
show you life's meaning
and help you through each night.

Our Song

If I could write a song about us
it would harmonize the beauty of the rising sun
as all the world awakens to it.
It would be about a love so strong it has grown
with each day passing.
I would have to tell the world of how your
smile and touch excite me,
how your gentle kisses ignite a fire within me.
I would have to tell them how walking side by side
with you brings out the stars above,
that when I close my eyes and dream,
my dreams are those of brilliant color
filling each night I sleep.
Explosive thoughts of you.
I would sing out loud how glorious
it feels to be held in your arms,
That all the wisdom you share with me
brings knowledge un-compared.
Our song could not be completed without telling
the world of our love, a love sent from
satellites and airwaves above
on golden wings as the stars sparkled their magic upon us.
Our song would be lovelier than that of a morning doves cry,
more delicate than any rose,
yet as powerful as the sun rays casting golden
ribbons down upon the earth.

"A FATHER'S LOVE"

Today I Went For A Walk

I have noticed how sometimes the most menial things can really be
symbolic,
You may ask what I mean or why I say this,
today I went for a walk,
I noticed the beautiful green grass,
the clear blue sky, the smell of summer in the air,
the smell of fresh cut grass, or how your senses can
smell if a light spring rain is coming.
I realized taking a walk is menial and many people do it,
but it was symbolic because I realized I love to walk,
it makes me happy and sometimes it give me ideas for my writings.
It just allows me to think, and to find answers,
by taking these walks I made a difference,
I changed something, I changed myself.
I gave myself the wisdom,
and thoughts which I could write down into words
for others to enjoy,
something I have always dreamed of doing.
I can be perfect in my own way,
now you ask what is perfect, no one truly is.
To me perfection is when I am the happiest I can be,
when I can accomplish something I never thought I could,
now that may not be your idea of perfect,
or your friends, or anyone else's for that matter, but for me it is.
I remember where I was a year ago,
no self esteem, in fear, suicidal, lost and alone,
and it was then I made a change.
My writings are far from perfect, or is it wise or worth
being history bound, but it is perfect to me.

I might fall in the process at times while I take my long walks
through life,
but I will stand back up and start again and all will be perfect once
more.
Perfect in my eyes and my heart.
I waited for perfection, I found it the only way I knew for me.

Pick A Star My Love

I remember the nights we sat and talked for hours about our lives,
about the beach and the stars above,
making plans for our future together.

In my dream last night,
we sat on a lonely stretch of beach,
one small tear rolled down my cheek,
for a moment the rays from the stars captured that tear,
that ray faded as did we,
what remains is a warmth that no one can extinguish.

Promise me on a clear night you will walk on that same beach,
you will pick a star, and I'll meet you there,
it won't be the easiest to find,
or the brightest in the sky,
but pick one that radiates to you as our love did once,
hold it close to your heart and never forget where it is,
for it will light your path in life forever.

Pick a star my love,
and maybe when all is right we will meet again
on that glorious sandy beach,
Pick a star my love, reach out your hands to me,
and I will meet you there.

Promises And Broken Dreams

A strong crisp wind sends chills down her body,
freezing cold,
her blood runs slowly through her collapsing veins
bleeding to death inside,
there is no stopping it,
a Course of pure white skin overlapping bones,
no strength left to move,
She lay there, tears rolling gently down her cheeks,
she knows in her heart and her weary mind the time is near.
Her eyes begin to roll back into her skull
her body slowly goes limp,
with no movement at all
her lifeless body grows cold and weak.
She no longer feels pain,
her heart and soul torn from her for the last time,
she lay there in a peaceful rest,
he enters her room, a room filled with white lace and red roses,
the smell from the roses overtakes the room,
her beautiful soft skin blending into the white satin sheets.
Her long silky hair flowing gently down her sides
as if she were a portrait in his dreams.
He begins to walk slowly towards her,
bends at the waist to kiss her,
her lips are moist but very cold to the touch of his,
she does not move, she no longer lives.
Tears rush from his eyes as he takes her into his arms,
slowly picking her up, holding her lifeless body close to his,
for the last time he kisses her,
she is finally safe and at peace with herself.

A darkness falls on this night, there are no stars shining,
the moon hides behind many gray clouds,
he holds her in his arms until the dawn breaks,
rocking her, whispering to her that it is okay that she goes,
softly laying her down upon the bed
turning to walk away he looks back one last time to see her,
quietly he closes the door to the room of his princess, his love.
The room of white lace and roses,
of Promises and broken dreams.

Radiate

My eyes weep with sadness,
though they still sparkle green color.
My heart ache's with pain,
though it still feels love.
My soul slowly falls into darkness
though it still sees a small star shining in the distance.
My mind has thoughts of giving up
though it still thinks and hopes.
My hands tremble fearfully but I hold them out to you.
My legs weak, but I still stand proud.
I am my worst enemy at times and
my largest storm to defeat.
Your friendship and words to me
bring me one step closer to defeating that storm.
From the moment we spoke a bond formed between us,
two souls in search of answers,
two hearts lonely and scared,
crossing paths between millions of people.
I ask you my friend,
look to the Northern skies and see
that the tears I shed have given way to the sun,
follow the path of the rainbow they formed,
for it leads to my friendship and trust,
each color representing those I hold dear to me,
add your color and become on of them
together with all the colors you will radiate.

Nothing is good or bad, but thinking makes it so.

William Shakespeare (1564-1616)
Playwright

Sand Pebbles

Here we shall unwind
amongst the sand and waters edge,
we can lose the strands that bind our souls and our pasts.
We can dance under the moons shadow,
naked for all to see,
Letting go of all that holds us from being free.
We can weep openly at memories that haunt us,
and unfulfilled promises scattered
through out our lives.
Here, amongst the sand pebbles and the
moons shadow, we can disown the
years before this, and we can search
for new strands to bind our hearts.
Dance amongst the stars to
new memories that we make.
An unquenchable thirst we both have
longed for.
Something so undeniable, complex,
as sand pebbles, dancing, and the moon,
have brought us new beginnings.

Trapped Inside

She sits in darkness at the rivers edge,
thousands of thoughts rushing through her mind.
Days filled with her own uncertainty,
scrambled images racing through her mind,
tears falling like a slow summer rain,
seeming to never end these days.
She has shed enough to overflow the rivers she now sits by.
The night breeze blowing softly on her face,
the moon full and radiant in all its glory above her.
She is trapped within herself,
trapped with her own destruction.

Someone

All of my life I have searched for someone who would
make the stars shine bright each night, someone who would
make each waking day bright and sunny,
with a warmth not found elsewhere but his loving arms.
I have searched for someone in my life who would make me
smile and laugh every day,
someone who would make me feel cherished,
and to give me a lift when I was down.
Someone who would help me step forward when I hesitate to do
so.
Someone who would hold and comfort me through the many
storms
life throws our way.
I have wanted someone to listen when I needed to
release my fears and hurt,
someone to guide me through difficult times
or dance with me and hold me close,
sometimes that peacefulness and silence is all I needed.
You my dear have done all of that for me,
you have opened your life and arms,
given me the love I searched for.
Now every night and every sun rise I need you here with me,
I love you, I am only complete when you are beside me.

My Life With You

Days and nights are so completely fulfilled.
My feelings are expressed openly,
with you I have nothing to hide.

My heart belongs to you,
hold it securely and carefully in your hands,
you are the only one for me.
As you hold my heart gently you will begin to see,
its filled with love like no other,
and in your hands is where it wishes to be.

I never once thought I could love again,
but with time you have proved me wrong,
You have helped me in so many ways
and your kindness and friendship
have helped me to become stronger.

Where once an emptiness filled my heart,
and tears filled my eyes,
you managed to fill the hollowness,
and to wipe away the tears left behind.

Voices Of Evil

Darkened skies fall upon the earth,
a silence overtakes her resting place,
fog creeping through the forest,
swirling around her body,
angry voices over powering her thoughts, demons,
words he has spoken to her
so ugly and full of hatred,
and evil voice trying to control her every moment,
her tranquility.
This control he has, this evilness,
causing her unbearable pain,
mixed up thoughts and actions.
Her mind seems to spin like a child's top,
spinning, spinning, seeming to never stop,
with her hands she tightly clenches the sides of her head,
screaming at the voices she hears,
the evilness that has taken control.
Depart from her soul and her mind,
let her have peace and serenity.
Let her find her way,
give her back her sanity, her love for life.

"PERFECT REFLECTIONS"

Waters Edge

Watching the waves of the ocean as they
crash against the rocks.
The tide once more coming in.
Feeling the coldness of the water
rushing over your feet as you walk
barefoot down the shoreline.
Turning slowly away from the waters edge
looking upward.
The evening sky turning from a beautiful blue to different streaks of
oranges and reds.

Imagine yourself,
weightless, floating amongst the stars,
seeing all the worlds beauty.
Feeling nothing but a peaceful serenity.
Protected from all the wrongs that man himself has created.
Hopes that the moment never ends,
that reality doesn't take the purity,
the freshness of this very second.

Seize the moment,
hold it in your thoughts if you wish.
let it guide you through each night that comes about.
When moments come that you feel you cannot step forward,
remember that peaceful drifting feeling of
walking on the waters edge.
Remember the song of the winds as they blew past you
and crashed the waves onto the shore.
Remember the fresh scent of innocence you felt
that day.

The world is full of happiness, and plenty to go round,
if you are only willing to take the kind that comes your way.
The whole secret is in being pliable.

Jean Webster
Daddy-Long-Legs
Dover

Thinking To Much

Remembering so many times that I walked in his shadow,
so often remembering the bad times in our lives,
why do we constantly think about trying harder,
giving more, loving more,
Being less than who we truly are.
So many times I wonder why I even take the time to think so much.
why I can't give my mind and thoughts a break,
let them rest for an hour a day.
Most of the time I wonder why I wonder.
Why do I waste time thinking about being positive
and less time actually being it.
If one thinks about it long enough he will see
how silly it really is to be thinking all the time.
I love to sleep even though I find it hard to,
sleep gives my brain a rest,
unless of course I am dreaming.
I sometimes find myself crying in my sleep,
and then I wonder why,
or I think about the dream I had and try to figure it out
in my thoughts.
I think to myself
why do I try so hard to make sure people do not
figure me out, or get close to me,
why do I keep my mouth shut,
why not speak my mind instead of muffle my sounds.
How can I sometimes despise people
but yet long for human contact.
Why do I run and hide, why do I hurt myself,
why??
Thinking!!

When Shadows Fall

A child with eyes blue as the ocean,
her hair flowing like spun silk, resting on her shoulders.
skin so delicate and pure, untouched.
She lay quietly on sheets of white satin.

The sun falls in the distant sky,
trees casting shadows across the yard,
stars forming in the darkness.
I stand at her bed side
the moon glows brightly,
shining through her window.

When shadows fall upon her wall
small cries pierce through me.
Kneeling next to her she explains,
the shadows on her wall scare her,
"looking" I see disfigured forms about her room.

I bend down and kiss her delicately,
whispering mom is here,
close your eyes my dear child,
the shadows will fall from sight,
there will be nothing left to fear.

I lay next to her
holding her small fragile frame in my arms,
her eyes softly close and she drifts off into a dream,
an innocent smile forms on her lips,
for she fears no more,
she no longer cries
for she now sleeps under the loving arms of her mother.

Wish Upon A Star

Through out my life I have wished upon many stars,
watching the skies at night
searching for the one perfect star to wish upon.
I would sit at my window,
the scent of burning candles filling the room,
the light from them casting shadows of odd shapes and forms,
I know someday when the right star shines brightly
that my wish I make will come true.

Have you ever wished so intensely that you can vision
the entire thing in your mind?
I can see the gentleness in his eyes,
but yet we have not met.
I can hear the peacefulness I get inside from his words,
but yet we have not spoken.
I can feel the tenderness in his touch,
the softness of his lips,
and we have not even met each other.

My heart will know when I see him,
even though it is fragile right now.
At times in much sadness,
and times it feels like breaking.
I know the time will come that it will be healed
and I will find him through the stars.

The clouds begin to clear,
the stars again shine brilliant sparkles above,
shinning in all their beauty for the world to see.
In one brief instant a flash passes my site as I search for the perfect
star,
a shooting star trails of sparkling colors trailing behind it
and Instantly I make my wish again.

I Wish To Myself

I wish to be myself,
for everyone to accept me for who I am,
but most importantly, for me to accept myself.
I wish to be loved,
to be cherished by one special person.
I wish for all the anger to stop,
to quit fighting and hiding within myself,
sometimes I wish to be everything he wants me to be,
everything I never could or can be for him.
I wish for happiness,
for perfect days filled with sunshine,
and nights filled with bright stars that light up the sky each night.
I wish to have someone to share this all with,
someone with warm arms to hold me when I am sad,
or comfort me when I am in pain,
for small children to always have smiles upon their faces,
for rainbows after every rainfall.
I wish for a peaceful state of mind,
I wish to see the beauty inside of me that others say they see.
To give of myself freely to him.
I wish for him to see how much I love him
and to know I never want to hurt him.
I wish for his own peace of mind.
I wish he could see the man I see.
As a child I remember the chant
Star Light, Star Bright,
Pick one of my wishes and make it come true tonight.

Yearning To Be In His Arms

I lie under soft covers,
the breeze from the open window swirls
your essence throughout the room.
My mind wanders off into thoughts,
thoughts of the man I admire and love.
Your face glistens out in my vivid imagination,
the softness of your eyes has the remarkable
power to make me smile.
I yearn to be in your arms to be
in your mere presence or to gaze at you
from across the room.
Your kisses more pleasant than the morning sun rise,
more pleasant than a chocolate sundae with whip topping,
Kisses more pleasant than a night sky filled with sparkling stars.
Hands so gentle, although
masculine and strong from work.
A smile that calms the storms inside me.
How lost my soul seems when you are not near,
how my heart aches for your every touch.
With every breath of air I breath I wish you were here with me.

Hiding From Those He Loves

Will he every come out of the darkness,
out of the locked world he has placed himself in.
Will he come out from behind the mask he wears
and will he show himself to me and all those that love him.
Let me see your inner strength, your inner weakness.
Talk to me in a voice I can understand.
One by one let the demons go that haunt you from your past.
Break free of them forever.
Behind the barrier you put up there is a beautiful and caring soul.
A man of courage.
A man that has strength to survive and has done so.
Without you opening that barrier and
turning on the light I cannot truly know you.
I cannot help you see the beauty of this amazing world we live in.
You cannot enjoy completely the purity of my love for you.
You hide from all those that know you.
I know it scares you to let them see that you hurt,
but that is all part of what makes each of us special,
it makes us wise and allows
us to be who we truly are.
I am not scared of the man that hides inside the darkness of you.
for the man that I see in front of me is
much more frightening to me.
No longer hide from those of us that love you.
Open and let the sun shine in your world,
let us not judge you but show you that we all
have dark pasts to forgive.
Move forward with me and enjoy a brighter world.

When you don't know what to do, walk fast and look worried.

Paul Dickson
Writer

I Found My Way

With my head full of dreams,
and a heart full of love
it was just a matter of time that
my dream came true
and I found my way to you.
I can't imagine any greater feeling
than waking next to you,
or falling asleep in your arms.
If I had to live life without you I would,
but it could never be as wonderful
as living with you.
When I feel I cannot go forward
you hold out your arms and comfort me
and my tears slowly seize
as your thumb gently wipes them from my cheek.
My answers all seem to be right here with you.
Everything I have looked for in life and more
lies in your heart and your eyes,
but most of all it is the way you allow me to be myself.
You do not judge me, or try to change me.
I cannot imagine my dreams or my life without you.
If these words are all I can leave you with,
I hope they comfort you and they console you,
that they warm your soul.
For you have over flowed
my life with gentleness,
kindness, and a love
incomparable to any I have known.

Young Soul

Grow and show the others in this dying world your words
so that all can share and feel the beauty that
you have within your heart my friend.
So young so filled with love and wisdom,
grown with knowledge so far beyond your years.
The words you speak and write should find the
hearts of so many others.
Look at what others will miss without ever seeing them.
Your kindness and wisdom coming through in rhyme,
the emotions you hold and carry astonishes me.
You have had so many barriers to break through,
many walls built of stone,
you have let your written words carry you through as I have.
Let others see what I have known for so long.
Let them know that life has many challenges
and that we can all overcome them.
Hold your head up proudly and never feel ashamed.
Let your words flow off your fingertips as do mine.
Let them drift like the wind and I as others will cherish them.
They have given me strength as I am sure they will others.
You my friend are more a part of me than you can ever imagine,
your words have released an inner being in myself
and have broken down a wall I too have built.
Share with the world the young man I have been so graced
to have in my life.
Never hide your words from others, for they are
who you are inside, they are what makes you stand out
amongst others and makes you a man far beyond your years.

This poem was written for a young man that became a very special
part of my Life,
even though we no longer keep in touch his friendship and support
of my writings will forever be held dear to me.

If We Shall Ever Part

IF we shall ever part my love,
I wish not for you to be unhappy or sad,
instead remember all the happiness we shared
and all the love that both of us have given each other.

I ask you, please never allow the sunshine to disappear in your life,
or let gray clouds take control.
Let the stars always shine brightly, even if it appears
there are none in the sky.

Remember our long conversations of future plans we made,
the long nights we sat and talked for hours.
The times we danced through the house in each others arms.
The support we gave each other through
so many difficult times.

No matter where you should ever travel in life,
my love for you will keep you safe,
it will always be the only love I'll ever truly know,
and it will always be eternal.
I promise you no matter where I am,
no matter our distance,
you shall always hold my heart within yours,
please hold it gently and protect our love and friendship.

A Young Man's Dream

Last night he dreamed of you again,
he heard you call his name..
His dream went back to memories of your beautiful smile,
and your eyes full of caring and tenderness.
you were so very young and he was so much in love.
You reached across and touched his face the way you
always did,
and in his dream you whispered, "I Love You."
He stood tall with pride, his head held high,
unbent from the years of turmoil in his life before the two of you
met.
When he awoke that painful night, alone
with only his tears to remind him,
he left you in his dreams where you shall always stay,
young, beautiful and forever his.
if only he could have that night back,
to feel your touch, to see your face, for just a little while.
But dreams of you are all that he has left to ease his lonely nights.
Your in the arms of angels and for that his pain subsides.
Memories of your gentleness will ease his troubled mind,.

To My Mom On Mothers Day

Today I want to write to you, a mother perfect in every way.
Today I want to pour in verses
the feelings that lay deep within my soul.
I want to capture all endless love for you
on pure white paper, infinite paper of my mothers heart
Today I write only to my MOM.

You are the most beautiful creation,
your tenderness contained in my tears of love shared.
You are the wisdom I have learned from and you walk
every day with me through life.
Your hair of silver threads,
your hands soft and caressing like little angels.
You are the rain that flourishes the earth,
you are my shelter through stormy nights searching for your protection.

Your hands are those of hard work but the true expression
of kindness you have offered to others every day.
Through you I learned kindness, gentleness and forgiveness.
Your voice is that of music to my soul, nurturing it
through my challenges on the road through life.

Although time has aged your endless beauty,
and walking has become slow,
your wisdom grows within me and your soul never ages.
You are my perfect model of what I wish to be.
You will follow me through the roads life leads me,
and you will forever be the greatest mom in the world.
Happy Mothers Day.

She's Gone To Heaven

She has gone to heaven,
but he needs her here today.
His heart aches and his tummy hurts.
he needs her right away.

At night he cries and calls her name,
but she is no longer there to hear his pleas.
Someone tell me please is Heaven far away?

She hasn't been gone that long,
and she needs to come back home,
He really needs to reach her,
and hug her one last time.

Someone hit her car that night,
they say she slid on ice.
And now she is in Heaven,
and he suffers through each night.

So please can you give him a number he can call,
to reach her in heaven?
I know it would help his tummy if he
could talk to her one last time.

Sometimes in the night he can feel her touch
and though he knows she's gone
he misses her so very much.

He reaches out for her and feels her arms around him
in the middle of the night,
but wakes to no one there.
Last night when he was sleeping he knows he felt her kiss,
her sweet gentleness.

So if anyone has the number to heaven
please pass it on to him,
I promise he will call her to give her one last kiss,
and in his dreams he will keep her
as she was always his.

It is better to have loafed and lost than never to have loafed at all.

James Thurber (1894-1961)
Humorist

Slipping Away

No one can see the pain inside of her,
A soreness, an ache that she hides in her heart,
her mind.
She cannot let it go, nor uncover it for all to see.
She does not know why she has these insecurities,
this fear of those around her,
She just knows it is consuming her every day,
It hurts her, scares her to let it burn deep within,
but she is afraid to let it go,
she is afraid she is slipping slowly away.
The mask she wears to hide beneath,
keeping her safe from letting everyone know her true inner fears.
Her smile is false, her happiness a joke,
it is all just an act for those around her.
She wishes someone could see beyond all the falsehood,
But, to do that they have to care,
they have to understand her inner most fears and thoughts,
those thoughts waiting to explode.
She is afraid of rejections, humiliation,
afraid of not being accepted by others,
afraid of not being good enough, or loved enough.
She just sits back and plays her part,
Mother, wife, friend, daughter, sister.
Never truly understanding who she really is,
she slips away slowly in front of their eyes.
Slips away from herself as well.

Intimate Thoughts

Possessed by violent passions,
is this the moment, is this eternity?
In a half deepened sleep
intimate thoughts of them,
loud sirens rushing past her window,
the wind whistling as it blows through the leaves outside.
Silence overtaking the world around her,
she lay quietly with only her thoughts.
Her imagination and dreams will go as far as her mind allows them
to.
His strong but gentle hands embracing her,
a calm masculine voice echoing the words she so
desperately needs and wants to hear.
His last kiss lingering on her lips,
the quietness of his love she can still taste upon them.
She lay listless in their room, their bed,
his scent embedded into the sheets she now wraps herself in.
Her thoughts wander off, remembering how beautiful it was
to lay there in his arms,
tightly holding her, protecting her, falling into a deep sleep in his
arms,
awakening in the very same position that they fell to sleep in.
tangled in sheets with his arms around her.
What consumes her now?
Intimate thoughts of him left behind.
The mystery of their sweetness and passion.
Drifting like the moon as night hours pass into daylight.
In their bed, their room filled with the smell of him.
She remembers each memory as if it were a shooting star in her
head.

Her eyes burst open, her body filled with passion they once had,
her heart beating the echo's and pain of the love she lost.
Her thoughts, her memories, her dreams are all she has to hold.
She no longer feels his warmth at night,
his fresh smell lingering throughout the house,
his laughter that filled each room with joy.
She no longer feels.

Broken Love

When we first met I never thought
of ever saying goodbye.
Our first dance, our first kiss,
felt like they would last a lifetime.

For so long the thought of losing you
broke my heart,
I couldn't bear us ever being apart.
The love I thought you lacked,
communication was never there,
but I kept trying, I kept loving you.

Many years past, many memories forgotten,
I tried to make you someone you were not,
someone I wanted you to be.

Broken dreams, broken love,
but now we can hold onto friendship,
it is only up to us.
Once lovers, Once man and wife,
can a friendship form that never existed before?

The Silence Speaks

Two hearts separated from one another,
each of them desperately searching for the other,
a chance meeting of the two,
eyes locked on each other,
the silence speaks.

Together the two learn of each others needs,
time heals their past wounds,
laughter and love fill their hearts,
together they become one.

Speaking often of their dreams, their fantasies,
Never for a moment doubting the other,
time passing and their words to each other begin to lesson,
each finding different paths,
different directions to take.

Years passed by and their hearts now beat a separate rhythm.
Knowing the pages of their love have turned,
that like all story book romances there is always an end.
an ending not always happily ever after.

Silence and loneliness speaks,
with time it now speaks different words,
different emotions.
A sadness of separated hearts,
separated love.

Dreams Tucked Away

So often I sit and wonder what your heart is feeling,
where do I fit into your life and
will I always be just a friend or am I more.
My heart cries out to you but you do not hear
my tears as they burn my cheeks and fall to the floor.
The days that we talked for hours have become so
far and few.
A part of me feels empty for I know I have
lost you to someone else,
I will forever remember your gentle voice,
your laughter and the way you made me smile each day.
A sadness now fills those smiles
and tears have overtaken the sparkle
in my eyes that you placed there.
Knowing I may never feel your lips touch mine,
or your arms hold me tight while I sleep,
Or seeing your smile as I wake in the morning,
devastates me.
All these dreams I shall tuck away and keep safe in my heart.
So many words unspoken through out the years.
So many feelings expressed through only written words.
I can only Pray that you always smile and remember me,
and your heart always saves a small portion for me.

Essence

Laying beside each other,
the room filled with the aroma of incense
swirling heavily throughout.
Two minds, two hearts connected.

His hands caressing her thigh,
a gentle distraction at best.
Shivers run deep within her,
enticing her and telling him to continue onward.

Warmed in each others embrace,
tasting the sweet nectar of each others kiss,
each undressing the other with their eyes.

Her flesh soft as silk,
damp with expectations of what is yet to come.
Her hair delicately laying on her bare breast,
tantalizing them as his touch does.

They begin to explore every aspect of seduction,
tasting each others flesh,
roaming and exploring each others bodies,
entwining each other in the sheets below them.

Her nails dig deep into his back
as he enters her,
drawing her closer to him
and her mouth lusting for his kiss.

Her screams of enjoyment,
her hunger for him finally fulfilled,
collapsing in pure ecstasy.

Nestled together,
locked in each others arms for the night.
Their essence fills the room where once
incense swirled.

There is nothing we cannot live down, rise above, and overcome.

Ella Wheeler Wilcox (1850-1919)
Poet and journalist

I Am Not Simple

Accept me for who I am,
for what I believe in.
I have thoughts, beliefs,
inspirations, goals,
just as you do.

Accept me without conditions,
don't push me out of your life,
don't leave me standing in darkness,
alone, cold, lost.

Accept me
for I breath the same air you do,
I walk the same paths in life as most,
I sing when the sun shines,
I cry tears the same as everyone else.

Accept me,
I am no different than you are,
One can't change the other,
nor should we begin to try.

Accept me as human,
as one friend to another,
accept the changes in my life,
for changes are inevitable.

Accept me,
I am average,
I am me.
I am the voice of millions
around the world afraid to speak.

Accept us all as individuals,
as people.

"THE MORNING BLUFFS"

I Found A Place

I found this place,
a place where my feelings were no longer ignored,
where they mattered.

I found this place,
a place where once again the skies were blue,
the nights sparkled with stars.

I found this place where my expressions,
creativity and thoughts flowed freely again
and they were all accepted openly.
Where I feel no boundaries,
and there is nothing I cannot explore or do.

I notice in this quiet place
I sing again, even if I am off tune.
I hear the words of songs and
the melody again.

People actually see me for who I am,
for what I wish for in my life,
and they accept that person
without stipulations.

I found a place,
a place where my heart is once again filled,
where my voice sings out laughter,
and my mind explores all options.

I found a place of serenity,
a place of peace,
I found myself.

No Songs To Sing

Each day passes with out melody,
without harmony.
My mornings filled with deep sorrow,
frustration.
The radio plays but I hear no tunes.
My mind blocks all expressions of joy,
happiness, love.
My thoughts now are incomplete,
scrambled.
Laughter and smiles
come to me on cue,
hiding from all my hurt,
pain.
Every day is a routine now.
There are no songs to sing,
no verse's to hum.
I am not happy,
I need something more in my life,
unsure of what that is,
confused,
walking around dazed.
Nothing is clear.
I stopped thinking,
feeling,
years ago.
I was a body and flesh walking
without a heart,
without a purpose in life.
So many thoughts,
no time,
pretending,
hiding within.

Falling

Nothing changing,
she fights the darkness,
the daylight.
It suffocates her,
leaving her in more pain,
leaving behind black and white,
no colors.
She is afraid,
afraid to be alone,
afraid to be with people.
People she loves.
Getting buried in darkness,
her own emotions,
absorbing her every thought,
trusting no one,
her world day by day crashing in on her,
falling down around her,
ripping away any protection she feels,
any security,
falling, falling,
deeper into a dark pit
of desperation.

If Tears Could Speak

If tears could speak what would they say,
they would softly whisper, "I'm sorry" in every way.

If tears could speak what would they say,
they would whisper, "I love you" in all the right ways.

If tears could speak what would they say,
they would quietly tell you, "you let me slip away."

If tears could speak what would the say,
they would ask you, "why you couldn't wipe them away."

Missing You

When she sits alone in the darkness of the night,
missing you deeply,
she closes her eyes and remembers your smile,
your deep brown eyes staring across the room.
She thinks back to the first day the two of you met,
your patience, understanding,
the laughter in your voice that she loved to hear.
She thinks about how she felt that day,
a warmth no sun could give,
a connection with our past, our present.
What she now sees when she looks into your eyes
is a beautiful soul, a gentleness,
a love so pure and true for her.
She sees what she has become.
He blindly helped her to once again see, to feel.
She thanks you for all you have given her,
for all he has done.
She does not know where she would be
if it were not for you.

Regardless of circumstances,
each man lives in a world of his own making.

Josepha Murray Emms
Playwright

Today, Tomorrow, Forever

Restless at the end of each day.
Relaxed by the comforting of his hands.
Without hesitation his words soothe her pain.
He vanishes her fears with the warmth of his eyes.
He is always there at her side.
The thought of ever losing him frightens her.
Without him her heart would be empty.
Her life would be filled with darkened days and sadness.
When he speaks his voice draws her to him,
an uncontrollable hunger to hear more.
Just being with him gives her a peacefulness.
He is as kind to her as a gentle summer breeze
delicately blowing across her face.
The comfort he gives her nourishes her every thought.
This man is everything to her.
He is her heart, her soul and her life long dream.
He is her today, her tomorrow, her forever.

Step Forward or Step Back

A strong sting left behind,
the red bruised glow she carries with her,
eyes swollen from tears of pain.
Her battered and torn soul.
Names called through out her life.
Days pass, silent years go bye.
Esteem taken from her,
does she belong anywhere?
existing with pain and anger.
The road ahead, dirty, dusty and long.
Rebuild, reformat life's dreams.
Strength, can she find it.
No tears, smiles alone.
Do you know her name?
Would you see her if she stood in front of you?
Heart opened, eyes a glare,
reaching, searching, finding each step harder.
Looking back,
seeing years past.
Does she step forward,
or does she step back?
Being secure where she was,
or unsure of what lies ahead.
Head spinning, answers await.
Would you know her,
would you hold her,
would you offer her your hand?
Can you be strong enough to understand,
or will you judge her like all others?
Push her away for her views are scattered,
her mind somewhat delusional.

Her heart still beats, her breath is still warm,
she is human, emotional,
just lost in that next drink.
She was a possession,
an ornament, a maid,
an object for his pleasurable desire.
Does she step forward,
Does she step back?
Do you know her?

I Love You

Forever and always my prince you shall be.
Smile and love me and we shall be free.
Our love for each other will keep us strong,
there will never come a day that it will feel wrong.

Jamie

You brought laughter to all those that knew you,
your smile brightened every day we had together.
The silly things you said and did,
your life with us, your family, ended to soon.
You began to drown in a sea of hurt and darkness.
gone, nowhere to be found, lost,
buried deep beneath the earth's crust.
At some point you lost your will to smile,
no one heard your cries for help.
A lonely night on a dark stretch of road we lost you.
When the music plays
I now cry tears of sadness for I did not
get the chance to tell you of my love for you.
The happiness you brought into my life and into
my family. I miss you.
So often I think of you,
I hope your at peace,
that you see what you brought to so many.
You had a great joy for life.
My tears will forever flow when I think of you,
for there is and always will be a part of my heart
buried with you.
Hold it and guide it from above,
point me if you can down the path I need to take.
catch me when I fall
and again point me in the right direction of life.
Someday I will join you and we
will once again laugh.

My Children

The sweetest moments I recall
will forever stay locked within my mind.
I speak of the moments with my children
by far the sweetest kind.

I watched my children learning,
and watched them grow each day,
becoming independent,
but never straying far away.

I watched each step they took,
and held their hand when needed.
I gave the love a mother can only give,
but made mistakes along the way.

I hold those memories tightly,
and cherish each and all.
Memories are so precious,
and I remember each and every day.

Too soon we turn and our children are grown,
childhood to adult.
In a mothers eyes it is
the shortest journey ever known.

Time does not impair the bond
between a mother and her children.
Even though we must let go
and let our children search
for a destiny of their own.

I pray I gave them all I could,
and showed them all my love,
a tenderness and lovingness,
to carry through their lives.
One which I hope they share
with children of their own.

I gave them wings to soar with,
and a purpose in this world.
I loved them with compassion

as best I knew I could.
The years have passed to quickly,
my children are all grown,
a new road emerges
and I find myself alone.

I now can only tell them,
each road we take teaches us,
sometimes the curves are sharp,
but each has a lesson for us to learn.

Never feel you have lost direction,
just look up to face your fears,
reach for the goals you have strived for,
and someday you will be proud
of what you have accomplished through life.

The qualities within you
will guide you through each day,
with this I want to tell you,
there's no better day than today.

My Mothers Love

My mothers love, no stronger bond on earth
a precious unconditional love created
when she gave birth to each of her children.
Her love is forever strong, it never changes with time,
and when she is needed most,
that is when her love shines.
All of our tears and heartaches,
the days we did not know which way to turn,
she was always there to guide us.
When her days on this earth are over
her love will live on through each of us,
passed down from generation to generation,
a love she gave so freely without hesitation or conditions.
When I think of her, I think of her smile,
her strength, her courage, and I am so very proud
to be her child.
She always lets us know there is nothing
we cannot accomplish.
She lives her life in kindness.
Giving so much love to us all.
She has shown me what It means
to be strong and face my fears.
Thank you Mom for the gift of being your child,
and for the gift of your love.

Sweet Thoughts Of You

Sometimes when I take a look at the world around me
I get so confused,
but all the confusing thoughts disappear when you walk
through the door and I see your smile.
I forget all my worries and my heart begins
to race with excitement.
Sometimes I feel overwhelmed by life
and sometimes I just do not know what to do,
but, you hold me and everything seems
right again,
your voice comforts me.
If we could look into a crystal ball and predict or see
our future, I know I could never understand it all.
One thing I do know, I'd be lost if you went away.
My days would never seem as bright as they
do with you here by my side.
As I wake each morning I long to look
over and see you asleep next to me,
wanting your arms around me,
wanting every minute, every second to be with you.
We all have this special way of being happy,
the love I have for you is mine.
Nothing can compare to that.
If I had to spend one day without you
it would be the longest day of my Life.
My day would have no sunshine, it would
be filled with an overcastting of clouds, and the
night would be filled with a horrible emptiness.
If I get the chance to spend my life with you,
I would try only to make your days
happy and filled with sunshine.

I would always be there for you,
standing proud to be next to you.
I would tell you how much I cherish you
and the love you offer me.
If you look into my eyes you will see my heart,
soul, body and mind and they are yours forever.
Sometimes I'm elated and hopeful,
and sometimes I'm down and blue,
but never a moment passes that my love
for you is not true.

Steel Cold Eyes

Sometimes when I look into your eyes
I see a coldness,
a hurt that you caused yourself,
why do you hurt yourself with past memories?
Why do you live to have eyes of cold steel?
Let me love you and help you,
I can see your pain from the past,
I can feel it pulling us apart,
I also can understand it.
I know you hurt,
I have seen your tears,
I can see it every day in your eyes.
Dark and cold like steel,
like your mind at times so very sad.
Do you understand the pain you feel, the hurt,
the emptiness you cause yourself.
In a way you push those that care away,
the way you sit alone,
or the way you avoid life and its beauties.
Don't you know I love you?
Can you feel my love for you overflowing?
I know this place your in,
a dark cold place surrounded by brick walls,
keeping everyone that loves you at arms reach.
I've been there.
You may find it safe but it will
swallow you alive.
It will consume you.
I beg you to struggle within and be free
of that world, that dark cold hell you are in.

Please let me in,
let me help you break free,
let me stand by you and show you a warmer Life,
better things to do and see,
Please just let me love you.

"CREATIVE EXPRESSIONS"

My Friend My Savior

You were the one that made me smile,
your words gave me hope and encouragement,
I could call and you would be there,
you would offer your hand and your wisdom,
my tears you would ease.
I came to you one day with my fears,
with my dreams and fantasies,
you told me I was someone special,
and offered me your friendship,
I came to you on deaths door,
weak and pathetic,
your strength kept me from falling,
falling into a deep and eternal sleep.
Your hands reached out to me.
I began to gain strength,
I began to find all the answers I desperately needed.
Finally finding who I am and want to be.
Knowledge and strength grew each day,
respect for myself lead me in new directions,
each day, each month that fluttered away
I wondered where that friend went,
the friend that kept me sane, that kept me alive,
the friend that showed me and taught me who I was.
Could I be complete in this world without her,
without her guidance and her friendship?
Could I continue to grow and find answers along the way,
or would the emptiness of losing your friendship
leave me back where I started?
Where are you my friend, why did our lives take different directions,
why have you walked away,
a friendship should not hurt like this,
it should not just disappear.

Once you held my dreams for me,
you kept them safe until I could find them again.
Where are you my friend, come to me once again,
enjoy the beauty of life I have found,
smile at the life you saved.

Slipping Into Forever Darkness

When will her tears seize to exist,
is it possible that she will never wake from this darkness,
a darkness that has consumed each waking second,
every breath of her life.
Feeling trapped in her own thoughts,
scrambling inside her head,
beating like hammers against her skull.
Darkness,
scattered, trapped dreams.
Hell searching for her soul.
Will she ever stop seeing his words in print,
she tries desperately to fight back into reality,
she has lost all sense of gravity.
She wonders will she ever wake from this nightmare.
Will the darkened skies every open
to bright radiant blues.
So many dreams shattered,
fighting to awaken from this cruel nightmare
the one he has put her in, falling deeper.
Slowly slipping from reality into a forever darkness.
Lost in the dark with only visions of her lovers
last words to her,
wondering why as she slips farther,
farther into a lifeless being.

Endless Dreams

I'm not exactly sure what I do from here
I have no idea what is beyond
the doors of what I call home,
a place where I have grown,
learned, and loved.

I despise the nights,
I toss and turn beneath the covers,
my dreams seem endless.
and my mind just runs in circles.
All the control of my life I thought I had seems lost,
My mind, my faith,
my sanity all seem non existing now.

The hope I once had in my dreams,
and my mind are gone.
There is nothing left to motivate me,
my children gave me the will power to go on,
but they are now gone.

I am heading on a downward path
that leads to a dark space,
my breath steadily ceasing,
gasping, unable to catch
even a small gasp of oxygen to inhale.
I've lost myself for sure.

Struggling,
I try to tell myself to care, to love,
to fight and have hope,
my mind fails to listen,
there is a silence,
the day has come to say my final good-byes
to all those that I love.

My Dearest Children

As your Mom I can sometimes see your pain
a pain that others do not see,
I know the hurt that is there without
you even saying a word.
I wish I could take it all away and leave you without
the burden you carry so deep.
I haven't the miracle nor the magic wand to wave,
but, my ears and heart will always be open to listen,
This I can promise you.
You have been through so much in your life in the past years.
Heard tails that scrambled thoughts in your mind.
You have seen what happens when love dies,
and worlds are torn apart.
This a promise I can make, I swear it with all my heart,
My love for you is unconditional and it shall never end,
with time we all shall heal.
I've made mistakes, I am human too,
said and done things I regret.
I can't undo the pain I've cause,
can you please forgive what you can't forget?
I know I have let you down, its not how I meant it to be.
I meant to keep my promise to all and stay a happy family.
Knowing the pain my children hold within,
the hurt of a broken home,
and their hearts filled with despair,
my pain does not out weigh theirs, it aches because
I have hurt the ones that I love the most.
Please get through each day my precious children,
have faith that time will heal.
Don't hold your anger deep inside,
nor hide the pain you feel.

For I know one thing that is true, it's
that you can be sure that sharing troubles
and the hurt you feel with those you care for and love,
is the only way you will endure.
I love each of you with all my heart,
and I am proud to call you mine.
Things will improve I promise you
all it takes is love and time.

The Art Of My Madness

Mind racing, words forming,
painting with words,
weaving thoughts back and forth,
some have rhythm,
others may not rhyme at all,
some colors mixed
no sense of recognition,
just no sense at all.
A brief moment of experiences
painted black and white,
Emotions,
some threaded delicately,
substance may not be there,
changing directions in the middle
of a stroke.
Portraits painted in words,
images in your mind,
you define them,
warped, loving
stories of mankind.
One brief message on a page,
millions of meanings,
words of little merit.
Secret passages to escape,
solitude, love installments,
feared heart, darkened
words flowing like blood,
with love, pain becomes poetry,
inner demons escape staining
the painted words,
soul escaping, trapped within these words.

Stabbing pain, driven, captured
with pen and paper.
Black and white,
eternity within my reach,
fear becoming action,
explosions within, silence changing.
Searching dark moments,
finding light,
can't be real, there is no light.

Etched In My Mind Forever

Blind eyes not seeing,
bones wrapped in loose flesh,
I walked beside you for so many years,
my eyes always looking downward.
My mind he never got to know,
my heart he let go.
Laughter he never heard,
tears he never witnessed,
I became a shell.
Living behind a brick wall,
my ankles shackled with chains,
a weight on my unwanted heart,
I wandered aimlessly in a shadowed world.
Carrying scars, bruises, hiding the pain,
the marks upon my heart.
Watching you drink, kill yourself slowly,
taking steps deeper and deeper
into your own self destruction.
You didn't see me slipping away,
with each day, each year that passed bye.
You never realized the full horror of the situation,
I became a figure you never seen,
lost in another drunken state of mind.
Dinners alone, movies to watch,
self esteem gone, heart lost.
You never seen my anguish,
my hurt, for you were lost yourself,
lost in past memories.
Demons gnawing at my heart,
tearing my soul apart,
lost in the pits of despair unheard by those around her,
A picture left etched in my mind and yours forever.

*The hardships of life are sent not by an unkind destiny to crush,
but to challenge.*

Sam E. Roberts

Passion to Live

It's been some time since I left
the home I lived in for much of my life.
Depression has kept me in a non existing world.
The time has come to evaluate my past.

I look back and what do I see,
failure, discontentment, insecurity in myself.
As I walk through my thoughts I
begin to drown in my tears of
feeling rejection from those I love.
My own rejection of myself and who I am.

I dredge up things which I now know hold me back,
I try and focus on qualities I have and
find only the ones I lack.
I cannot change the past so now
I imagine it is my future that I need to
rearrange.

My mind is so obsessed with the opinions of
those I love, of what they think I should be,
or how I should act.
If I am to change the future of my being
those days must be gone forever, those thoughts
extinguished from my brain.

I am unique in my own way,
my mistakes have made me who I am today.
People can say what they wish.
I know who I am and it shows in all I do and say.
I reflect in the hearts of my friends and family,
of my children.

My passion for life and the things I love to do,
my laughter, my giving heart all apart of me that
I wish to never change, it can never end.
I now know it is who I wish to be.

Past scars, mistakes I have made,
the pain I have caused others I love,
none of these will ever fade away
but they are there to remind me
and to strengthen my days ahead.

You may not understand that now
but someday as I grow to be a better person
you very well may.
Sometimes I am afraid of the future,
this I will admit,
This is my life, my world now,
and I deserve a peaceful state of mind.

I shall step away from all that has kept
me in the past.
Move forward to all I want to experience
and be.

I Walk A Silent Path

I walk a silent path,
leading through the tall crooked oaks,
the only sounds are that of my feet shuffling through
fallen leaves,
broken branches underfoot,
the sun's rays piercing through the path of a fallen tree,
the earth seemingly quiet.
Each step goes nowhere, as my life has,
I seem to lead myself in circles,
finding nothing of satisfaction these days,
unaware of my existing inner self being.
The peacefulness, the beauty,
only if I could open my heart and soul again
it may let me be free to witness what
others have already seen.
As I walk and the sun sets in the distance
I find myself crying tears of remembrance of
a woman once so naive to others,
never understanding but always giving what I can.
When I find myself needing the will to survive
and the strength to stand and face challenges
my thoughts wander off to words He so long ago spoke to me.
Words that for years crushed every emotion I could
muster up inside myself.
I remember that day as clear as a sun filled summer sky.
When I needed his strength he ignored my cries,
Just a simple hello would have eased some pain at
that moment in time.
Here I am, walking a silent path that now seems
to lead to no where, feeling alone,
feeling scared of what the future may hold for me,
not knowing where I can go or who to turn to.
Wandering silently.

Tormenting Thoughts

Painful words she read now travel through her mind,
spinning around over and over.
Help her understand why.

She cannot breath, excruciating pain in her heart,
she can't believe he hurt her this way,
she prays each day that what she read is not true.

Her heart and soul aching with confusion,
unaware of where this will leave them,
tormenting thoughts tearing, ripping her apart inside.

What has she done to deserve this pain,
to deserve such betrayal from someone she loves,
what more did he need or want from her.

Did she not give him all he needed to be happy,
was she a burden on his life,
or just a play toy for the moment.
Tormenting thoughts consuming her.

The Mountains Cried

Under a bleeding moon the mountains cried aloud,
weeping as tears rolled quietly down the rocks,
flooding every emotion, every being below.
A frozen image of the earth's fire,
the mountains and sky crying out to those
that so desperately wish to change the
beauty of this amazing creation.
Can we forgive or understand those
that take all that is so elegant in nature and
burn it to the ground, or those that cut green
branches that reach for the sun.
The crystal blue streams of water that flow delicately,
the sound of the waters flowing softly over golden rocks, the smell
of fresh spring rain as it falls to the virginal ground beneath us,
the sounds of thousands of species roaming
and singing melodies to their partners and offspring.
Advancement in the world, technical knowledge that
has so quickly taken over what some call a precious life.
Do these professors of knowledge know the history
of the morning dove and its mate?
The bond of a lifetime not to ever be separated by any means
other than man's hands or their own natural death.
The site of a male morning dove resting on the eggs of his off-
spring,
yes the male, unlike the species called human.
The mountains as they cry streams that flow gently down its val-
leys,
wild flowers that grow amongst the hills and fragrance the earth,
grasses and foliage that feeds the same creatures playing in
the meadows below. Plants, meadow grass, trees that spread
a pure fresh oxygen over this land of ours.
Simple lessons no longer taught to our young.

The beauty of where all life began so long ago,
the amazing simplicity that man took and under his hands
destroyed for knowledge, technology and construction.
Give my grandchildren knowledge,
let them know what life offers each of us,
teach them, let them grow, but do not take from them
the most precious gift of all, Earth's own simple but
perfect beauty. Let the mountains cry, the moon bleed over all of
us,
for maybe then we shall have life's most knowledgeable lesson of
all.

To My Daughter

The bond we have between us
will never go astray
for I hold you in my heart each day.
Sheltered by my love for you,
protecting you from harm.
If I cannot have you here with me,
what better place to be.
Our paths will surely meet again,
and we shall never more part,
a sweet reunion it shall be,
a brand new life to start.
We will walk down streets
made of sparkling gold,
making up for the time we have lost.
Remembering all the times we shared,
they are the sweetest I have known.
I could never pay you back for the
precious love you have given me,
and words alone are not enough,
to express my thanks.
I will just tell you I'll not forget
the kindness you have displayed,
the times I needed comfort the most,
the times I needed help,
your love is what you gave.
To thank you would not begin to be enough,
to love you unconditionally for as long as
I walk this earth is what I can give.
I love you my child,
my daughter.

Silent Pristine Path

The sun quietly sets,
streaks of light glisten off the freshly fallen snow.
No one can hear her, no one can see her
as she walks a silent path alone tonight.
Her tears fall with the memories of the past,
freezing instantly as they trickle down her cheeks.
A clearing in the trees ahead of her allows her to lay and rest,
she lays her tired body down upon the pristine white snow,
her swollen eyes look upward,
viewing a beautiful star filled sky.
She wonders if the memory of her will fade,
like a ship on the ocean in a foggy summer night.
Will her words drain from their thoughts,
or will they leave an impression on one simple person.
Will those who knew her remember,
will they remember the beauty of her heart,
the love she gave freely to those in need.
If so, let them see her spirit glitter off the dusting of snow,
or soar above them upon eagles wings.
Streaks of majestic purple, midnight blue, or gentle yellow,
she will be there looking back,
she will hear the cries whispering to her,
the laughter enlightening her.
Faintly smiling her soul and heart content with who she is,
who she was.
She drifts off into the distant sunrise,
tears forming in her heart,
as she leaves her memory behind.

Behind every great achievement is a dreamer of great dreams.

Robert K. Greenleaf (1904-1990)
Business leader

Path Of Love

The taste of delicate tears that slowly drop to my lips,
salty, unforgettable, a taste I will forever remember.
Each tear that falls, each that falls slowly to my lips
reminds my heart of the pain in loving you.
Many say love is not suppose to hurt.
I once believed in those words.
In reality if we love completely there is always some hurt
along that path of love.
No one human can live up to all of our expectations and dreams.
Those that love us sometimes put us at such high regards
that they set us up upon a pedestal and do not see our faults,
yes we all have faults.
It is when one of our faults are displayed for our lover
to see them, and only then is our love truly tested,
many fail that test.
Do my words touch any part of your thoughts,
when I dig deep inside my soul and find the words
I so desperately need to say. Do you hear them?
Do you feel the tears I shed through them?
Can you understand them and let them touch you within?
If you can, it is then that you can truly give all of yourself to love,
and then you can become one together.
For now I write my words to you,
I open my thoughts, my dreams, my expectations for the future,
My heart is open, my arms stretched out waiting,
my dreams are those of two together in love,
and I share them only with you.
Remember I am not perfect.
I have faults as do all of us,
do not place me upon that pedestal and witness my fall,
for I am human.

My book of words will never close to you,
for if it every shall, then all my words seize to have meaning,
and if that day shall ever come,
my heart will die a thousand deaths.

Our Legacy

I want to make a difference in your life,
in spirit and in need.
I want your life to shine so bright
and burn inside of me.

I want the world to look at you
and see the love of me,
that all I am reflects
from within your eyes.

May all the love I give you
be a legacy for you.
May it guide you through the future,
and forever carry through.

Let the words of love I offer,
and the gentleness of my touch,
show you life's meaning
and help you through each night.

The Heart Of Jamie

Jamie was a gentle simple soul,
his time with us was taken painfully,
he gave his best to those he loved,
and he did so with laughter and friendship.
I know he did not wish to leave,
life to him was all he knew, survival.
At times he spread himself way to thin.
His laughter would fill the largest of rooms.
If your day was dim and you felt no need to smile
he could walk into a room and nothing
could seem more wonderful.
When his time came to an end the laughter stopped,
no longer were our rooms filled with smiles and
the love of life he brought.
Though I miss him each day, I believe he
hasn't really gone away.
All the love he gave will carry on in each of us.
We shall all keep his laughter alive, and his love for life as well.
Our love for him will never die,
tears often still flow from all of us at times,
but the memories he left us shall in time take
the tears and replace them with smiles.

Family What is its Meaning

Over so many years there seems to be different views
on the true meaning of family.
We all have them, what is the correct term of the word
and who is right or wrong or do all the meanings that so many
different people view all mean the same.
Now we could look the word up in a dictionary or a Thesaurus,
and find that it means many different things,
from relationships to households and to offspring.
We can believe that it means only our blood relatives,
and how far back does that go into history.
We can believe it is our immediate relatives only.
Through years I was one that believed it only stood for
my parents, siblings, children, grandchildren and yes those that
our children married.
Don't get me wrong, what ever one person believes is not
either wrong or right.
We all have the right to believe what we wish that is what makes
this such a great country.
Who am I to ever say someone is wrong in their views, or who is
right.
I have learned many things in recent years,
many which I believe have made me a stronger and a better per-
son.
I believe a family begins with all those we love
and all those we hold dear to our hearts.
If that is children, friends, co-workers, siblings,
parents and yes partners in life.
My dear Sister gave me a wall hanging several years back,
It reads, Having a place to go is called HOME,
Having someone to love is called FAMILY,
and having both is a blessing.

Until recently when I truly read what it said I too believed
what many do, but since I have understood its meaning.
A family does not have to only consist of children, parents,
Grandparents, Grandchildren, siblings or even husband and
wife. It can consist of all the above and also include friends and
partners in life.
For some of us as life goes on our journeys change,
and what we thought was family only increases with each change
and it fills our life with so much more insight and pleasure.
I am very blessed to have them all, and, they are all my family no
matter the distance of miles that may separate us, or how often
we talk with each other.

Do Not Be Fooled

Do not be fooled by the face she wears
for she wears a thousand masks.
She gives the impression to others she first meets that she is secure.
That happiness and confidence is all around her and that she truly
needs no one in her life.
Do not be fooled by the words she types,
underneath the real woman hides, alone and confused and in fear of
her own sanity. She is afraid that deep down inside where she
allows no one
else to see, that there is an empty shell, nothing, that she is no
good to or for anyone, even herself.
He seen but was not fooled, he then rejected her.
She has told you everything, or has she?
Listen to what she is not saying, is she genuine in words that she
does not speak?
Can you help her, can you hold out your hand to her?
Every time you were kind, loving and gentle.
Every time you tried to understand because you truly cared.
Her heart began to grow wings, very feeble wings, but wings.
With his sensitivity and power of understanding came faith.
He alone released her from a shallow world of uncertainty.
It will be no easy task for him, the closer he gets to her the blinder
she becomes.
He told her once his love was stronger than the walls she built.
Will those strong hands break through those walls,
for inside them lives a scared child.
A child that looks endlessly for hours into her mirror,
what she sees within the glass she fears the most.
She stands wondering who she is,
what mask will she decide to hide behind today.
Do not be fooled, Do not.

"NATURE'S BEAUTY"

Wishes

I wish to be myself for once,
for everyone to accept me for who I am.
For me to accept myself.
I wish to be loved not for the person who pretends,
but the person that hides beneath.
To be cherished by one special person.
I wish for all the anger to stop,
for the fighting and hiding within myself to end.
Sometimes I wish to be everything he wants me to be.
Everything I never could or can ever imagine being.
I wish for peace,
for perfect days filled with sunshine and nights filled
with bright stars that light up the sky in brilliant colors.
I wish to have someone to share this all with.
Warm arms to hold me when I am scared,
or comfort me when I am in pain.
I wish for smiles on all children's faces,
and for there never to be hurt and pain in their lives.
For rainbows after every rainfall.
I wish for once to have a peaceful state of mind.
To see the beauty inside of me that others say they see.
To give of myself freely.
I wish for him to see how much I love him,
to know I never wanted to hurt him.
I wish he could see the man I seen.
For star light, star bright,
pick one wish I wished tonight,
send it to me on wings of a dove,
star light, star bright.

Remember, all the answers you need are inside of you;
you only have to become quiet enough to hear them.

Debbie Ford
Personal growth coach

In My Dreams You Shall Stay

All I need to do when
you are not with me
is to close my eyes
and imagine your charm,
your laughter,
your warm passionate soul.

Our love was that of
a clear blue stream of water,
constantly flowing,
never seeming to find an end,
At night when I am asleep
you come to me in my dreams,
we dance,
and sing to music on the radio,
Your arms gently hold me to your chest,
your lips softly caress mine.

This is my favorite time of the day,
my favorite place to be,
I feel safe there, I feel peace.
I never wish to open
my eyes and awaken,
for if I do you will be gone.

In my dreams you live forever,
we never part.
We lay in each others embrace.
There is no one to come between us,
no one person that can
destroy our love for each other.

In my dreams on this star filled night
I will keep you forever and we
shall never part.
It is you that brought
meaning to my life
and it is you that lives
within my soul
and my heart.

My Search

All of my life I have searched for someone who would
make the stars shine bright each night, someone who would
make each waking day bright and sunny, with a warmth
not found elsewhere.
I have searched for someone in my life who would make me
smile and laugh, someone who would make me feel
cherished and give me a lift when I was down.
Someone who would help me step forward when
I hesitate, someone who would hold and comfort me
through the many storms life throws my way,
I have wanted someone to listen when I need to
release my fears and hurt, someone to guide me
through difficult times or dance with me
and hold me close at times silence is
all I need.
You my dear have done all of that for me,
You have opened your life and arms,
You have given me the love I searched for and opened
up your door.
Now every night and every sun rise,
I need you here with me,
because I love you and I am only complete
when you are beside me.

Sweet Thoughts Of You

Sometimes when I take a look at the world around me
I get so confused,
but all the confusing thoughts disappears when you walk
through the door and I see your smile.
I forget all my worries and my heart begins
to race with excitement.
Sometimes I feel overwhelmed by life,
and sometimes I just do not know what to do,
but then you hold me and everything seems
right, your voice comforts me.
If we could look into a crystal ball and predict or see
our future I know I could never understand it all.
One thing I do know, I'd be lost if you went away,
my days would never seem as bright as they
do with you here by my side.
As I wake each morning I long to look
over and see your smile,
watching you sleep, wanting your arms around me,
wanting every minute, every second to be with you.
We all have this special way of being happy,
the love I have for you is mine.
Nothing can compare to that.
If I had to spend one day without you
it would be the longest day of my life,
my day would have no sunshine, but filled
with dark overcastting clouds,
and the night would be filled with a horrible
emptiness.
If I get the chance to spend my life with you,
I would try only to make your days
happy and filled with love,

I would always be there for you,
standing proud to be next to you,
I would tell you how much I cherish you,
and the love you offer me.
If you look into my eyes you will
see my heart, soul, body and mind,
are yours forever,
sometimes I'm elated and hopeful,
and sometimes I'm down and blue,
but never a moment passes that my love
for you is not true.

Her Mirror Image

She walks with grace,
the clapping echo of her shoes
heard for miles as she walks towards her reality,
her head hanging low,
her eyes fixed on every step she makes,
her mind wandering into insane thought.

For one brief moment she stops,
looking into the plate glass window of the store she passes,
her image she sees so differently than that which others see,
she stands in amazement at herself,
how easily it is to hide all we feel inside,
how easily we can add a hat or a certain dress
and our image to others changes.

It is only through her eyes she truly see's herself,
for she is the only one that knows
the pain she holds within,
if you see her standing there,
you see a small frame with a glow and a smile,
she sees an aged woman, in tattered clothes,
wrinkles deep from worry,
eyes blackened from restlessness,
a heart filled with emptiness.
Her soul fading.

Now look again,
do you now see the difference?

As long as one keeps searching, the answers come.

Joan Baez
Folk singer

Dad

As a young child in my fathers home
I remember the smell of grease as he would come home
from work each night,
The tiredness in his eyes as he would sit down at the dinner table,
There was this silence at our table,
My father was a stern man, and as his children we had this fear of him,
I am not sure today why we did,
We always knew his love for us.

Our home looked like a palace,
but we were far from rich with material things,
Our parents raised us with the riches so few today know,
a family bond of love, respect, and caring hearts.
The spring would come and the garden work needed to be done,
Side by side as a family we planted each seed to grow,
Sirens would blow for help in our small town,
and my father would rush off to do what he could,
the pride that I felt I cannot explain, even as young as I was
I remember I was so deathly scared,
what if something happened to him while he helped others.

You may ask why I write these words of my father?
You see, for the first time I see my father growing old and weak,
his health failing, today I seen him cry for the first time,
he hugged me goodbye and gave me a gentle kiss,
he sent me off with his love.
I didn't want to let go, for it was something
I so desperately longed for since childhood.
He was never one to say I love you,
today I heard those words and for the first time and
I truly felt his love.
There are times I feel I have left him down,
but I know even if I have he still is proud of me.

I called my father today, for the first time in my life
I did not feel that small child within me escaping once again,
He did not judge me, nor lecture me,
As I said my good-byes I felt tears slowly stream down my cheeks,
I so desperately wanted his hug once again,
It is odd to me that it took half my life to know that feeling,
I will thank God for giving me my fathers hug that day,
I shall never be to old to feel the love of his arms wrap around me.

I Love you Dad

Magical Merlin

He sits in the background of a crowded room,
not a soul in the room noticing him there,
Silently his magic begins to fill the room,
smiles and warm hugs all about,
the mystery of his words,
roaming through the hearts of so many,
the energy he so often shares,
the warm tenderness that he freely
spread to all those that love him,
and with all that he has never asked for anything in return.
he has been hurt by others as have many of us,
he trusted in someone that betrayed him.
Come with me, turn out the lights,
lay back under this star filled night,
hold my hand and I will comfort you,
Let those dark gray thoughts turn
to brilliant majestic colors,
colors so bright that not even one person
can touch them,
and dare they try, for I guarantee you this,
Your dreams, your soul and your magic charm
will not fade into darkness again.
Very few hearts as yours survive,
souls torn and destroyed by human touch,
only left to become angry pieces of flesh rotting,
no emotions, just hearts of stone, preying on
others.
Hold my hand and enter the room with me,
let them see two hearts willing to share,
unchained by their words and deceit.

It is my turn to give you strength,
to share with you the strength and compassion
you have so willingly given to others,
hold my hand dear friend, bring your magic
and lets spread our friendship, souls,
and love like star dust amongst them all.
If we can together entwine one of them in our web
of trust and our smiles, then my dear Merlin, we have
done all we can.

Written for my dear sweet online friend Merlin
"your magic will always live in my heart"

Lost

Lost,
A dark place,
her mind confused,
no where to go.

Running,
running from life,
from herself,
from the past that haunts,
Lost.

No destination,
no plans,
falling once again,
pain.

Searching for a hand,
medicine to ease,
thoughts crippling her,
cure if there is one,
finding nothing,
alone, lost.

Dazed,
day after day,
children crying,
scared of the unknown.
Lost.

The Day I Found You

When you walked into my life,
and you opened my heart,
I never dreamed you would hold the key
to a world I never knew,
a world of love and so much more.

Once I let you in,
how would I have ever known you would
brighten every day there after,
or make my heart your home.

When I see your smile now,
there is a beautiful view of dreams,
of hopes, wishes and a lifetime love.

When your arms are around me,
I feel what so many including myself write about,
a love so secure, so pure, so honest,
a love so real.

To only you I make this promise,
and you know you can always believe,
for as long as I live you will be all I will ever need,
desire or dream.

Perfection In My Eyes

I have noticed how sometimes the most menial things can
really be symbolic,
You may ask what I mean or why I say this,
Today I went for a walk,
I noticed the beautiful green grass,
the clear blue sky,
the smell of summer,
you know, like when you can
smell fresh cut grass or when you smell it in the air
that rain is coming,
I realized taking a walk is menial,
many people do it,
but it was symbolic because I realized I love to walk,
it makes me happy,
sometimes it gives me ideas for my poetry,
sometimes it just allows me to think,
and to find answers,
by taking these walks I made a difference,
I changed something,
I changed myself,
my way of thinking, I gave myself
wisdom and thoughts which I could write down into words
for others to enjoy,
something I have always dreamed of doing.
I can be perfect in my own way,
now you ask what is perfect?
to me perfect is when I am the happiest I can be,
when I accomplish something I never thought I could,
now that may not be your idea of perfect,
nor your friends,
or anyone else for that matter,
but for me it is.

I remember where I was a year ago,
no self esteem, fear, scared, suicidal,
lost, alone, and I made a change,
My poetry is not perfect,
nor is it wise or worth
being history bound like Frost,
or Angelo, but its perfect for me.
I might fall in the process at times,
but I can stand back up and start again
and all will be perfect,
Perfect in my eyes and my heart.
I waited for perfection, I found it
the only way I knew.

If one is without kindness, how can one be called a human being?

Sarada Devi

His Own Creation

Emotions spinning wildly through her heart,
memories and times shared.
Tossing from one side to the other in her mind.
Words spoken that cannot be taken back,
words that haunt her to this day.
So many things left unsaid as she cried in silence.
Many words he never heard, tears he never seen.
She hesitates, and wonders why she took him at his word.
Picturing his laughter inside as he fooled her heart and mind.
His words of honesty and devotion to her,
the same words he utters to so many others,
many women like herself hurting inside.
Women who gave him all they new in their hearts,
their dreams, fantasies, sorrow.
His soft gentle words spoken to each of them,
so clearly the same as they all now know.
Rehearsed like phrases in a book,
read to each of them with no meaning at all to him.
Memorized words like a childhood fairy tale.
So many of these women he has hurt have now turned
their hearts to stone, Pierced with his gallant efforts
to entice each of them into his web.
His words so well rehearsed will be
all he has left to remember, an eternal revenge
from them to him.
The hearts of these many women will mend and
another will show them the love they deserve.
The endless nights that he will sit alone can never
heal or be filled with anything but guilt.
The script he so delicately rehearsed and devotedly followed,
now floats with the wind through a cold bitter day,
a world he created for himself,
a world he can now caress and love as he sits each night alone.

A Mothers Love For Her Daughter

As I sit here thinking of you, I remember the day
I was blessed to have you.
A warm sunny day in August,
a day that filled my life with joy and happiness.

As the years have passed on,
you have grown to be a beautiful person.
A person of faith and love,
one with respect and trust and
a heart filled with love for others.

I have learned many things from you,
as I hope you have learned from me.
I trust you and love you unconditionally.
My love will always be here for you when ever you need it.
A friend I will be if you need an ear to listen.

You will always be a very special reminder to me
of what great things life offers us.
If ever there is a doubt in your mind just ask
and I will tell you I love you and how very proud of you I am.
I will hold you as I did when you were a small child,
I will wipe your tears from your cheek.
I will always be there to comfort you and guide you
if you need me to be.

If ever there comes a day I must leave this earth,
always remember I will be with you.
In the stars I will be watching over you and sending you light,
with the moon I will be sending beams in your direction
to guide you on your journey.
With the opening sunlight a love you will always have to
hold closely.

Take care my child,
listen to your heart and it will guide you,
make all your dreams a reality and never let any person
take them from you.
Most of all, be yourself, because you are a very special person.

I Love You..

When Love Is Right

When love is right,
you see it in each other's eyes,
you feel it in each others arms,
you taste it in each other's kiss.

When love is right,
you hold onto it with
your heart and soul and
nothing could feel more perfect.

No matter the distance
or the touch,
you can feel it.
It doesn't have to be in person.

One word can make all the difference,
and nothing can take that away from you.
No one person can pierce through it.
When love is right.
Nothing feels more right
than the love I have for you.

Remember Me

Remember me with a smile,
I will always be watching over you.
I am now in the hands of angels,
I look down at you and smile.

Remember the nights you comforted my heart,
the days you put laughter back into my life.
Do not cry for me, do not be sad,
for we found a love that so many search for.

As each day gets more difficult for me,
I hold onto the strength you shared with me,
the friendship you never once let go of.

Remember my words, my laughter,
the tears we often shed together.
Remember the beauty of my soul and heart,
for they will hold you close forever.

My one wish is that you never allow anyone
to take and destroy the beauty and love you have,
the wonderful soul you shared with me alone.

Make a difference in the world my friend,
let others see that life is precious,
that loving someone only brings joy to our life.
It does not matter what they look like,
but who they are inside.

Do not shed tears as I leave this beautiful world,
do not be sad at all,
for you have brought much joy and happiness to me
in days I no longer had the will to go forward it was
you that held me up.
You gave me courage to fight.

I have shed enough tears for both of us,
smile my dear friend.

Unstable Vengeance

On the edge of an unstable vengeance
that of ones heart,
stripped of tenderness, love,
the will to care.
Stripped of the desire to want or need,
slowly air drawn into the lungs,
released.
Heavy droplets of salty water,
sleek dark silence of everyday existence.
Every molecule of emotion ripped from within.
fierce aching, constant rage.
Wedged between walls of stone,
lodging themselves,
screams echoing through these damn stone walls,
uttered words without meaning.
Exploding each of the memories,
the betrayal of love and trust,
one by one haunting until they come loose and shatter.
Empty, suffering,
a river of tears flowing beneath the eyelids,
overtaking every ounce of life left in the soul.
A hollow shell.
The stench of destruction,
hatred and revenge now consume.

If

If life were a rainbow you would be my sun.
If heaven could be found on earth it would be in your smile,
If a single tear of pain fell over your cheek
it would overflow my heart with sorrow.
If the sound of a voice brings hope to a heart,
yours would make mine beat forever.
If strength ceased to run to my legs,
I could still walk with you by my side.
If actions speak louder than words,
then taste my lips and hear my souls desire.
If a dozen roses say I love you,
then let me plant a field of them for you.
If a kiss can slow time,
then making love with you would last forever.
If every you are lost or feel like you are alone,
look in your heart, you'll find me there.
If every you have doubts or are confused,
hold out your hand and I will guide you to me.
If a heart could speak,
mine would never stop talking to you.
If my love could be like the wind, it would pick
you up and bring you to me.
If I could pick a star from the nights sky that
would give you strength and courage,
I would pick the brightest one shining.
If I could find the end of the rainbow,
I could only wish that it would lead me to you.

One Day With You

If I could have one day to spend with you
I promise we would never get enough of each other.
We would hold hands, and walk the beach together.
The stars and moon shining in all there glory above us.
We would talk of our past lives,
talk about our present dreams,
but most of all we would enjoy the touch of each others hands.
If I could spend that evening with you,
I would cherish each minute that we were in each others arms.
I would stare into your eyes and
you into mine, we would know at that moment
that there was no other for us.
I would take each day and make it happier than the last,
I would promise you I would always be there for you,
never letting a day go by that I didn't say I love you and
how very lucky I am to have found you.
As life would have it we will never have that day,
for you have left and found yourself in the heart of another.
My dreams will never fade away.
I will hold the thought of us as one forever,
and I will hold you in my heart until I no longer exist.
My dream, my fantasies can not be taken from me.

Her Own Corner

She sits in silence, she ponders if love really exists at all.
Is there one person that can fulfill all her needs.
Will dark skies ever clear a path for the sun to shine
even just for a second.
Emotional betrayals holding her heart now.
Can she ever truly let go of the past or will she
remain there for ever.
Words come so easy for some of us but the
damage they leave behind can last a lifetime.
She wonders at times why she still exists.
Always feeling rejected.
always sitting in the background.
She can hide her emotions from all around her,
she can play the games so well,
but inside she can only be herself and bare all the weight
of her pain alone.
Gasping at times for air to breath,
feeling lifeless,
closing her eyes and praying they never open again.
That she would fall into an endless sleep,
holding only the dreams that she has left.
All that is right here inside her heart.
No eyes can see her now,
she hides well behind brick walls impassable to all,
shutting out anyone that dares to try and enter her world.
A dark room with nothing inside,
only a shadow curled in a corner.
Hiding her face in darkness,
collapsing at times into total mental exhaustion and
again wakened by confusion.
In her mind she is alone and
she will stay there for she finds no exit.

Thoughts To My Child

Life offers us only what we go after,
if we are not willing to explore new things
we shall never go forth and find ourselves.
We can sit back and watch life pass us by,
which I have for many years,
or we can take a step into an unknown space,
scary as that may sound and
explore options we thought did not exist.
We gain strength from finding who we are,
and from trying new things in life.
We would have never learned to ride a bike if
we had not taken the step and tried,
It may have scared us but we did it anyway.
This journey you have taken may
be difficult right now, but it will teach you, it will give you
strength and you will find peace when it is over.
If that peace is back here at home, or if it
is in a different area of the world
let your mind and heart
open to new experiences and find yourself.
For only then will you truly know who you are as
a person.
It is when you find your inner self, your inner strength,
that you can truly love yourself.
I carry your love with me each day as I wake,
I take it with me into my dreams and I know
that your strength from within will keep you safe.
My angel, when you can step outside yourself,
and you can like what you see, you will be happy.
See your beauty, your will and accomplishments,
with that I Know in my heart I have given you
the best part of me, and all the years and the tears have
so well been worth it to me. I see in you all
I have hoped you would grow to be.

The Rivers Edge

The sun sets in the horizon as I sit along the rivers edge.
The fragrance of freshly bloomed wild flowers fills the air.
The river is silent, as if it too lay to rest for the night.
In the distance an Eagle sores in flight,
searching for prey to feed its young.
I sit in amazement as to the beauty nature holds,
the peacefulness.

With the moon rising I lay back.
The stars slowly forming clusters all around me.
Sparkling diamonds above.
Shooting across the sky as I hear the faint
repetition of an owl screeching.

The night air begins to cool and
my thoughts begin to wander.
How is it possible so many never see this beauty I am
seeing, the elegance,
the enchantment and mystery of this night.
All lives answers lay amongst the beauty that the earth itself holds.
It is for us to stop and take notice,
for when we do it is then we will have our answers.
Simple pleasures of nature far out weigh anything of value.

The eagle in flight, the owl screeching,
the sun that sets every day.
The moon that never fails to rise or the
forever fragrance of wild flowers in bloom.
The rivers edge that I lay upon.
All priceless pieces of nature that man
is slowly destroying.

Letting Love Go

When we love someone completely we sacrifice our own wishes
and happiness to see that person whole.
That person will never know the loss or pain we feel when
we let them go to find themselves.
When we love someone completely and unconditionally
sometimes even though they love us as well,
they have to do something that they know will hurt us.
They must do it anyway to help themselves heal,
again it may be us that pays the price for them to be whole.

Sometimes the penalty we pay for loving completely
is the death of part of who we are,
then that part of who we love can live.
A love so deep and so strong that we alter ourselves.

If that sacrifice is to much for us to pay,
and if we have to force it upon ourselves,
then it is not truly love.

There is a stench of killing off part of who we are for love,
it carries with us forever.
And it is the price we pay for loving them.
Sometimes love means sacrificing all we know,
no matter the cost to ourselves.

Angry words and doings do not show love,
Silence sometimes holds more meaning.
They will never truly know the penalty we paid for loving them.
and we will never truly get over that love or its loss.

White Linen

I lay wrapped in white linens.
I have bared my heart for the last time,
emptied of its passion for life,
it's precious cargo.
Let it fade,
dissolve.

My skin silent without his touch,
the night falls
struggling to hold back, to breath.
I unwrap myself from the white linens,
forbidden flesh,
hands shaking.

I am told that I am loved by many,
but I sit alone with only my pen in hand.
My heart grows heavy,
so many promises.
I hear a voice calling me into a cold lifeless place.

I leave not only my friends,
but also a part of me.
A part that fears I will not be remembered,
that all my words meant nothing.

"CALIFORNIA RESCUED"

Her Friendship

On days when I feel so all alone
she hears my cries from words I type.
She knows my pain without even seeing me.
I close my eyes and I can feel her hug me.
I can hear her voice whisper, "breath".

How can anyone not know her friendships is real,
her heart as large and open as the ocean.
A love so strong that it never stops giving,
a laughter so sweet and genuine.
I call her my friend
but she is so much more to me.

When I find it hard to continue on
she hands me a little of her strength.
When I feel I cannot stop the tears from flowing,
she borrows me some of her laughter.
When my heart is broken and pieces torn from me,
she takes a part of hers and fills the emptiness I have.
When I build another row of bricks on the wall surrounding me,
its then she takes two rows down with her own hands.

How can anyone tell me
that you my cyber friend are not real?
You alone have given me so much in your words
than anyone has in person.

Your eyes have read my words and felt my pain.
Your hands have typed love and friendship.
Your heart, though it be thousands of miles away,
has felt each tear that flows down my cheek.

I've been let down so many times,
I am tired of hurting,
but you always believed in me.

You have always stood by me,
maybe not in person but I feel you there everyday.
comforting me and encouraging me.

Sometimes I believe you were sent to me for a reason.
You were given to me to guide me and show me
the road to which I am to take.
If you don't mind I would like to keep
you with me at all times.
I am sorry if I drain you of emotions,
or if I ask for to much,
but I promise you this with all my heart,
that with your love and friendship I will be strong someday.
When that day comes I will lend you my strength,
I will lend you pieces of my heart and my knowledge.

I can now only ask that you have patience with me,
that you hold my hand tightly as I make my choices.

Written for my dear friend Shelly,
without her support and love
I would not be alive today.

The Friendships He Built

Words flowed easily from his fingertips,
A smile most of us never seen but it
filled so many hearts with love and warmth.
There are no words that I can import that can reach the
hearts of those he touched.
Silently I can sit and reflect on the things he taught.
Many of us have our own beliefs of what kind of man he was.
The reality of words coming from people we have never met.
Many believe that closeness cannot come from these words,
but I for one believe they can.
Many believe closeness and lifetime friendships cannot
happen unless we can see, touch, smell or know every
aspect of a person.
This amazing man thought of his friends he made and
cared deeply for them.
Until the day he passed to a better place he never
gave up on any of them.
The friends that were to some only words on a screen
and not real.
So tell me how we can be so cold and not feel his love for us all?
He made promises to some he could not keep,
as I am sure some made promises to him as well and
could not fulfill them.
With all that was inside of him he did try.
He left us all with many wonderful memories,
I for one will hold him always dear to my heart
and I never met him, I had the chance.
He died with grace and dignity.
It is now his time to soar.
My heart as do many others grieve for him,
for a wonderful friend is no longer there
to comfort us or to make us laugh.

Soar my friend in heights far above,
let the wind blow softly and take you to places
where the sun never sets, and the air is warm.
Where flowers are in bloom year round.
Our hearts are filled with the memories of you.
Because of your caring heart ours will beat a rhapsody today in
your honor.
So fly my friend, let the wind carry you,
let the love we shared flow freely off your wings,
and sprinkle it through the stars and clouds
for all to share.

Written for a wonderful online friend
and one of the sweetest men I knew

The Storm

The winds howl and the storms inside her rage on
with all the pain and no particular course.
No relief insight as the storm rages on
day after day.
Red stained ground cover from the tears
that spill rain.
The storm raging on in a destructive path.
Slaps against her skin like hail beating the earths crust,
stinging flesh.
Release the pain,
break down.

"THE PERFECT FLORIDA SUNSET"

A Walk Along The Ocean Shore

A walk along the oceans edge
with stops along the way,
we pass the time finding shells and talking on the way.
Crystal blue waters rushing across our toes.
His gentleness is kindred to the moonbeams casting light upon
the waves.
As I brush against you I can feel your heart beating
like the ocean waves pounding against the shore.
The scent of you surrounding me,
an entranced state of ecstasy
where time and place simply do not matter.
Falling against the crystal sand beneath us,
catching our breath suddenly and closing our eyes,
the feel of your body against mine,
his gentle yet stimulating touch becomes
amazingly arousing, a kiss softly intimate,
waves rushing the waters edge.
She is now completely lost inside this delicious sensation.
Soft lips resting gently against hers, exploring
with urgency, she opens her mouth from his persuasive pressure,
bodies entwined and blending together perfectly,
plunging them into an explosive delight.
Hot kisses caressing her face,
Anticipating his every move,
Mouths roaming to exotic areas,
tantalizing her breasts, accumulating intense desire,
He becomes one with her.
Devouring each other,
engaging in private sensualities
as they lay under the moons glow against the sand,
basking in each others eyes.

Treasured Sorrows

Speak to me of all the days past,
what makes the man that stands before me now.
Treasured sorrows that you may have learned from,
or painted rainbows that engraved memories.

Let go of the past that has frozen your emotions,
warm the iced wounds that form your soul,
surrender them all to me and give to me
your ability to love with dignity and pride.

I'll hold you until your tears fall free,
absorbing all your pain.
Let me sing to you until all your fears are erased.

Together we can weave our lives to form
a beautiful blanket,
wrap ourselves in a peaceful content
that sets us both free.
We will find safety through our broken lives,
though they may seem scarred and helpless to
others they will be perfect to us.

Innocents Lost

He heard the phone ring and his heart began to cry,
his mind knew and screamed why,
imagining the last call from her he received,
now his eyes will no longer see as the last
precious breath was taken from her.
He lay silent at days end unable to sleep,
he wishes he had been there to take away any pain,
raising some barrier to protect her.
He weeps for you and wonders why you were
taken so very young.
He hopes that you felt no pain,
but in his heart he knows of pain you endured
through prior years.
If he could have taken the brunt of the crash
and saved your precious life,
He would have shielded you with his own.
To hear her laugh, her soft little giggle,
to love and be loved as she so freely
gave to him.
He will think of you as seasons pass,
from slow spring showers with endless tears,
to the horrifying winters cold that took you from him.

Her Thoughts Of her life

Quiet,
Shy,
chubby little girl.
No tears seen,
Fear,
scared,
unwanted,
alone.
Fat,
wallflower,
laughter from others,
name calling,
abuse,
sexual.
pregnant,
seventeen,
child herself,
married,
unwanted.,
drinking,
baby,
drinking.
accusations,
hatred,
angry words,
alone.
drinking,
Work,
broke,
alone.

Mistakes,
locked doors,
mocking her,
tears,
scared.
another child,
crying,
sleepless nights,
waiting,
watching,
slaps,
drinking,
bruises,
christmas.
Alone,
scared,
lost.
slashing,
blood,
hatred.
Insane.

You have your way. I have my way.
As for the right way, the correct way, and the only way,
it does not exist.

Friedrich Nietzsche (1844-1900)
Philosopher

The following sections of Poetry were written by me in
a learning experience with other online friends.

The group taught me it was okay to express my feelings and
that they didn't always have to make sense to anyone else.

I was given a word for the week and then took each letter of
that word to start a new sentence.

Several were printed in online magazines and
I am very proud of that.

Demonic

Demons lurk to destroy what they fear,

Eyes of black Satan piercing through every wall, every small crack,

Making contact and bursting into fire, destruction,

One flash of daylight burning their flesh,

Night falls with the stench of death floating through the air,

In each corner lies ashes of Satan's path,

Control taken by darkness, hate, greed and death.

IMAGINE

In a flash of insanity our world falls victim to terrorism.

Moments of silence and vigils held world wide.

Another day will pass with victims lost in rubble and families across the world waiting and wondering if their loved ones are alive.

Gallant efforts to save lives by many exhausted men and women.

Indescribable terror, fear, tiredness, and the heartfelt tears for those yet identified.

Never ending love is shown for our Country, proud and strong, One Country standing proud and united.

Existing now to prove our faith, our love and our freedom to find those responsible for this horrific act.

Diamond

Distant sunset, layered in crimson and white as the night air settles.

Inner Peace of mind and soul, as I know in my heart you are with me watching.

Another day comes to an end as I lay my head to rest once more.

My dreams tonight filled only with thoughts of our love and the longing to be together.

One soul, one heart, forever bound for an eternity.

November leaves changing colors, showing the end to another year and the beginning of a lifetime with you.

Dawn breaking, golden colors streak beautifully through my window as I wake,
once more the sun opens another day with thoughts of you,
thoughts swimming delightfully through my mind.

Summer

Somewhere in time his smile I will taste, his eyes will be forever
etched in my mind and his heart will be free to love me.

Until that day arrives I will dream of night skies filled with sparkles
of colored glass, sweet
drops of nectar nourishing the earth I lay upon.

Many have tried to enter the gates to my soul but the lock to enter
has many keys,
find the right set and my soul will be forever free to explore you.

My words will captivate your mind as yours will mine, our every
breath
our existence will be as one.

Entwining our souls, seeing only the beauty in each others eyes,
hypnotized by the warmth
of each others touch.

Rendering to each others needs, resting in a peaceful state of
forever love an eternity of two souls, two hearts, two bodies joined
together in one friendship, one love.

Question

Quietly I lay to rest with images racing through my mind of two entwined in each others arms.

Untouched by the world around them they can only feel the warmth each returns to the other.

Existing, yearning for each embrace.

Silent and breathless in each others arms, hands melted together as they fall peacefully asleep.

Their images planted in each others dreams like a freshly painted picture.

Intimate moments captured here for only those that care to imagine or question what is a perfect night of love.

Opening their eyes as morning breaks with memories of an enticing evening of passion.

Nothing surrounding them but reality and the joy of a life time memory captured in one black and white painting on the wall.

Whisper

Watching the streaks of orange and red as the sunsets deep in the horizon, his arms wrapped tightly around her.

Hesitating to let her feelings known, not only to him but to herself, for her heart has been torn so many times before.

Insecure, frightened, a mixture of emotions unexplainable.

Surrounded by the memories of those before him, refusing to let the future take hold, dwelling inside from pain inflicted by others.

Promises given but never kept, wondering will you, can you possible be any different from the rest.

Entwined in his arms she finds a warmth she has not felt for a long time, can she open herself up to him, shall she take that chance?

Resting her head upon his chest her eyes close, she finds herself releasing the past, the sun now completely at rest and the moon casting shadows down upon them.

Forever

Fear of the emotions she holds so deep inside herself.

Over time building walls so high that she did not let any human
enter her world.

Remembering the day she let him slowly remove each brick she
was hiding behind.

Eventually allowing her soul and heart to be free to feel again.

Very much aware of the safety she felt behind her own closed
doors.

Endless days and nights of your words to her bringing her back into
the real world,
out from the locked doors she would hide behind.

Reminding her each day that she is a very special person and her
heart needs
to be shared with all those she loves.

Manipulation

Many ideas of how one can take control of another's mind, but can they truly do so.

Anticipation of control, of the higher power one feels when they can turn things to their advantage.

Nothing stops their addiction to have their own way

Independence doesn't exist in the society or mind of such an evil-ness.

Perfection of the game, of the control of ones actions, thoughts, mind.

Utilizing ones ability to feel total satisfaction of the life of another.

Lowering their self esteem until they are completely under your control, until they have no mind of their own.

Anxiety of ones own fears that force their mind to try and change the thoughts and the ideas of another.

Temptations, evil in a sense, or so it may seem to the one that thinks they are in control.

Indifferent to the thoughts and beliefs of those around them.

Open to no other ideas than their own, their beliefs are the correct ones, the only ones.

Nothing else matters to them but to get their way at all times no matter the cost.

A Word from the Author

As I sit here night after night trying to think of things in my life that readers of my book would like to know about me I have a very difficult time coming up with anything, my mind seems to find a blank screen. Now, its not because there are no memorable times in my life there have been many, I find it difficult to talk or should I say write about myself. I turned to a dear friend for advice on the subject and he gave me his ideas, but, to me my life seems so ordinary, so much like millions of others. I asked myself to remember someone that I feel made a difference in my life or something that changed it drastically, so with that I shall begin to try and tell you, the readers, about myself. I can't sit here and tell you that I spent four years in college or some grad school. I can't even tell you that I was a great student through school. But I can give you some Idea of my life until now.

I was born July 26th, 1955, my mother always told me it was the hottest day of the year and I had to wait for that day to be born. I was born breach which only made my mothers labor even more difficult. Through life she would tell me I was born backwards and that I had been that way ever since, Odd, different ideas and thoughts I guess, she didn't mean any harm by her words. I was raised with three sisters and a brother, all whom live their life in Wisconsin, Packer Country, and they are all devoted Packer fans. See, I was born in Green Bay Wisconsin and lived most of my life in a small rural town west of there.

At the young age of seventeen I was married to first love. From that day on my life would and did change forever. I never had much of a self esteem, I always felt less than who I was and I always felt as if I never fit in anywhere. Now some would differ with that story but it is how I felt, until I was in my forties I didn't even understand why or that I felt the way I did when I was young. At the young age of eighteen I gave birth to my first born son, Michael David, even though he was a baby, a young child, the love I had for him got me through

207

some very painful times in my life. As the years went on I gave birth to another son, Corey Daniel and a daughter Kerry Ann. My children become the only reason I existed. The only purpose to my life.

As the years passed my self esteem fell to all time lows, I remember one day I had to ask my oldest son to leave our home, It was the most painful day of my life, I still cry to this day when I remember the look he gave me and the words he said to me that night. My son Michael had been my rock, my reason for living for so long, the one good thing I had done in my life, the one person I knew without any doubt loved me. That was the first day of a long battle within myself to stay alive.

Yes my husband was still there but he also had a problem of his own, a problem many people in the world share, drinking. For many years I sat up late at night watching out the window in fear, waiting for him to come home, or for the phone to ring and tell me he was hurt in an accident or dead. Now I won't spend time here putting down my ex husband, he is a wonderful man he just had a problem with drinking and I think in the long run we just got married way to young. I will always hold him in great respect and part of my heart will always love him.

My children all grew to be wonderful adults, I can honestly say that I never truly had any major issues with them or any trouble. My oldest son has given me three wonderful grandchildren which I love dearly. My second boy has had issues in his life but he has worked through most of them and is on his way to becoming the man I have always known he would be. Now, my baby girl, she is all grown up and beautiful inside as well as outside. I see so much of myself in her. When I talk with her now I can hear so much of the same issues I dealt with in her words, her voice, it scares me sometimes. She has become the one person I know I can always count on being there for me. I am truly very proud of all my children, and they are the greatest gift I have.

In my late thirties and early forties I started to withdraw from everyone, I started wanting to be alone with only my thoughts, I started writing my emotions on paper or typing them into small little verses or ramblings. For the longest time it was the only way I could understand how I was feeling, or the only way I knew how to let my feelings out without letting anyone else see my pain, my suffering inside. This is when I met my dear friend Shelly, the women that would in time actually save me from myself. As the years passed bye I became more withdrawn, more depressed, even to the point of suicidal. Yes I thought of many ways to end my life, many scenes I imagined but never acted out. In October of 2002 I picked up what my car could hold and I began a six month fight for my life. That road took me to the middle of Illinois, near St. Louis, Mo. and that is where I have since found my second home, my new life, and a peacefulness I have dreamed of for many years. A calmness inside, a respect for myself, and the knowledge to know I can make it in this huge world on my own if need be.

I have a love for animals and I give all the love I can to my three puppies, Jackson, Izzy, and the new puppy that still has no name, well we just got him yesterday so give us a break for now, I promise he will have his own name by Christmas. I enjoy almost any craft project you can teach me. I have found a great love for photography and I hope someday to have a better camera so I can continue my passion for it. All of the pictures you will see in my book were taken by me. I have had the privilege of working with the elderly in their homes, it has given me a whole different out look on life and getting older. I respect them all. So many of them are alone, forgotten by their family and children, so many have to learn a whole new life and it scares the hell out of them. As people get older and forgetful we call them the elderly, their children seldom come to see them, most of their friends are all ready gone. these people that have spent their lifes working to build our country and to just live out their life with respect and in comfort, forgotten by so many. These wonderful people that can't help that their are afraid, the life they knew no longer exists. The sad part to me is that the State pays me to go in and be their friend, their companion, As I have gotten to know so many of them I could only ask that some how I could have the honor to know I have made a wonderful difference in their life.

Made in the USA
Monee, IL
07 July 2026

56550069R00128